proclamation 2

Aids for Interpreting the
Lessons of the Church Year

easter

Bruce Vawter, C.M.
and
William J. Carl III

series a

editors: Elizabeth Achtemeier · Gerhard Krodel · Charles P. Price

FORTRESS PRESS   PHILADELPHIA

Second printing 1984

Library of Congress Cataloging in Publication Data (Revised)

Main entry under title:

Proclamation 2.

Consists of 24 volumes in 3 series designated A, B, and C which correspond to the cycles of the three year lectionary plus 4 volumes covering the lesser festivals. Each series contains 8 basic volumes with the following titles: Advent-Christmas, Epiphany, Lent, Holy Week, Easter, Pentecost 1, Pentecost 2, and Pentecost 3.

CONTENTS: [etc.]—Series C: [1] Fuller, R. H. Advent-Christmas. [2] Pervo, R. I. and Carl III, W. J. Epiphany.—Thulin, R. L. et al. The lesser festivals. 4 v.

1. Bible—Homiletical use. 2. Bible—Liturgical lessons, English.
[BS534.5.P76]   251   79–7377
ISBN 0–8006–4079–9 (ser. C, v. 1)

Contents

Editor's Foreword

Every Sunday, "the first day of the week" (John 20:1), celebrates the resurrection in the Christian church, but from apostolic times the church has also marked with special celebration the two primitive feasts of Pascha and Pentecost, borrowed from the Jewish Passover and Pentecost. "Pascha" comes from the Greek *pascho*, "to suffer," from the Hebrew *pesach* or "passover." Thus originally Easter was a feast of redemption; it celebrated the passion, death, resurrection, and ascension all together; its lessons were those of Hosea 6, Exodus 12, and John 18:28—20:31. It marked the deliverance of Christians from bondage to sin and time and death into the "glorious liberty of the children of God" (Rom. 8:21) and "the eternal kingdom of our Lord and Savior Jesus Christ" (2 Pet. 1:11). In short, it was an *eschatological* feast.

In the first two centuries, Easter was celebrated by a vigil held from Saturday evening to Sunday dawn, the blessing of a lamp or lamps, lections interspersed with chants, a sermon by the bishop, the baptism and confirmation of neophytes, and finally their participation with the faithful in intercessory prayers and the Eucharist. The new converts were believed to have been made members of Christ and of his Body at one time, by means of the sacrament. They "put on Christ" in Baptism, were "anointed with his Spirit" in confirmation, and were incorporated into him by participation in the Eucharist, thereby becoming members of his eschatological kingdom.

Catechumens prepared for such membership by preparatory fasts and daily exorcisms, but for fifty days after Easter, all penitential observances such as fasting and kneeling at prayer were forbidden, the time being a continual celebration of entrance into the kingdom.

In the fourth century, however, Cyril of Jerusalem transformed both the meaning and celebration of Easter. Because he lived in the holy city, Cyril introduced the idea of commemorating the events of our Lord's passion, death, resurrection, and ascension at their original or traditional sites, and the whole of the Pascha took on the flavor of *historical remembrance*. Palm Sunday, Maundy Eucharist, Good Friday, Easter, Ascension became separated from one another, as historical commemorations, with the cross dominating in Western liturgies, apart from Easter and Ascension Day. This has had a profound effect not only on the liturgy but on Western theology as well.

Easter has always been a movable feast, after Jewish Passover custom, but Western Christians from the first placed it on Sunday, while Asian Christians (known as Quartodecimans) continued to celebrate it on the Passover date of 14 Nisan. It was Pope Victor, at the end of the second century, who finally imposed the Sunday observance on all.

The death of Jesus, apart from his resurrection, has been made the dominant emphasis in this book. Lent and Holy Week fill up the time, while the celebration of Easter is limited, in most churches and despite the season of Eastertide, to one Sunday in the year.

In addition, the treatment of the Passion and resurrection from a memorializing point of view has tended to relegate them to the past, as events involving other people rather than ourselves. In short, we have lost our identification with and our part played in the stories.

One of the most serious consequences of this loss of identification with the stories has been the growth of anti-Semitism. The Jews as a whole have been frequently and vituperously blamed for the death of Jesus. Thomas Aquinas even spoke of their "deicide," their murder of God in Christ; and church liturgies, passion plays, and literature (for example, Chaucer's Canterbury Tales), have reinforced that festering hatred of the Jews which finally spewed forth in the poisonous gas of Hitler's "Final Solution." But we can blame the Jews for the death of Christ only by exonerating ourselves. "The Jews" in the Gospel according to John are a symbol of the world's and our own unbelief, and unless we confess that we all crucified our Lord, we will never see that he died for *our* sins and rose again for *us*. We Christians are the wild branches, grafted into the root of Israel, says Paul (Rom. 11:17-18); we have become members of the commonwealth of Israel, writes Ephesians (2:11-16). We were all there at the foot of the cross; our deeds caused Jesus' death. But the resurrection is the forgiveness of those deeds and the promise of new life, and finally, says Paul, Jew and Gentile alike shall inherit its benefits (cf. Rom. 11:26-32; 14:11-12).

Our exegete for this volume is the distinguished teacher, editor, and scholar Dr. Bruce Vawter, C.M., chairman of the department of religious studies of De Paul University, Chicago. Professor Vawter received his doctorate from the Pontifical Biblical Institute in Rome. He has held teaching positions in nine seminaries or universities, has served editorially on numerous scholarly periodicals and committees, and is the author of several dozen articles and numerous books, the latest being *On Genesis: A New Reading* (1977).

Dr. William J. Carl III, our homiletician, is assistant professor of homiletics and worship at Union Theological Seminary in Virginia. Dr. Carl is a graduate of the University of Tulsa, Louisville Presbyterian Theological Seminary, and the University of Pittsburgh. He has taught at the latter two institutions, as well as at Pittsburgh Theological Seminary. He is an editor for *Homiletic*, has written for *Interpretation*, and is the author also of the homiletical interpretations in *Epiphany*, Series C, for Proclamation 2.

Richmond, Va.   ELIZABETH ACHTEMEIER

The Resurrection of Our Lord
Easter Day

Lutheran	Roman Catholic	Episcopal	Pres/UCC/Chr	Meth/COCU
Acts 10:34–43	Acts 10:34, 37–43	Acts 10:34–43 or Exod. 14:10–14, 21–25; 15:20–21	Acts 10:34–43	Acts 10:34–48 or Exod. 14:10–14, 21–25, 15:20–21
Col. 3:1–4	Col. 3:1–4 or 1 Cor. 5:6–8	Col. 3:1–4 or Acts 10:34–43	Col. 3:1–11	Col. 3:1–11
John 20:1 0 (10–18) or Matt. 28:1–10	John 20.1–9	John 20:1–10 (11–18) or Matt. 28:1–10	John 20:1–9	John 20:1–18 or Matt. 28:1–10

EXEGESIS

First Lesson: Acts 10:34–43. In this chapter of Acts Luke is dealing with a subject dear to his heart, the universality of the salvation proclaimed by the Christian gospel, encompassing Jew and Gentile alike. It is a notable episode in his history of the catholicizing of the church, which in Acts moves by degrees both geographically and in ethnic composition away from its Jewish origins to a liberating movement throughout the entire Greco-Roman world. This pattern is the working out of the Lord's promise and mission to the apostles that, in the power of the Holy Spirit, they should be his "witnesses in Jerusalem and in all Judea and Samaria and to the end of the earth" (Acts 1:8). The discourse attributed to Peter here is delivered on the occasion of the conversion of Cornelius, the first out-and-out Gentile to be admitted into the church. Prefaced to it is an introduction presenting Peter as leader of the Judeo-Christian church of Judea, Galilee, and Samaria, consolidated and on the brink of its outreach to the Gentiles (9:31). Peter visits the outlying filial churches, and miracles attend him, as they did Christ before him. By means of them and the apostolic preaching, the church grows larger. There follows a presentation of Cornelius, a centurion of the Italian Cohort: Luke is probably thinking of the Cohors II Italica Civium Romanorum, composed of Italian volunteers, which was stationed at Caesarea, the Roman capital of Palestine (10:1–8). To the vision accorded this God-fearing man corresponds one given to Peter while visiting nearby Joppa (10:9–16), a vision which equivalently proclaims the end of the Mosaic dietary laws. This vision is to condition Peter for the meeting

9

with Cornelius (10:17–33), during which he is brought to recognize that as there is no divine distinction between acceptable and unacceptable foods, neither is there any divine distinction between acceptable and unacceptable people, that rather God's desire is for all of them to be joined to him in Christ. Following the discourse is a little "Pentecost of the Gentiles" (10:44–48), an event which effectively puts the divine seal on Peter's decision. The Gentiles receive a visible manifestation of the Spirit recognized by the Jews to be quite the same as that pentecostal coming of the Spirit (2:1–42) which had given birth to the church in Jerusalem. Therefore they are baptized in accordance with the manifest will of God.

This passage fits in with a series of artistic devices employed by Luke for theological purposes. The literary form of the discourse itself, an evocation of the primitive Christian kerygma usually ascribed to either of the early apostolic giants, Peter or Paul, is one of those Lucan devices. It is in Luke's interest to represent Peter, the first acknowledged leader of the apostolic Jewish church (Gal. 2:7), presiding over each stage of the subsequent development of Christianity into an ecumenical religion. Any number of Luke's historical interpretations can be and have been the subject of critical controversy. The extent to which the discourses, in particular, simply reflect the theology of Luke or do retain authentic memories of the early Christian proclamation continues to be the subject of intense scholarly debate. We might think, for instance, that in the light of Gal. 2:11–14, if Peter's is the doctrine that is presented in Acts 10:34–43, it was a doctrine that he rather easily forgot and rather quickly. We must be content to take the theology of Luke in the spirit in which it was offered, as the interpretation of the meaning of the church as it was envisioned by one who spoke for a major tradition of all those which have contributed to the canonical New Testament.

The discourse may be perceived as constructed in five parts and as following a chiastic structure, that is, a structure in which the middle part (vv. 39b–41) has the central significance, flanked by two developmental sections which correspond to each other (here vv. 37–39a on the one hand and v. 42 on the other), and included within an equally corresponding introduction and conclusion (vv. 34–36 and v. 43 respectively).

In this catechesis, the seventh discourse of Acts and the first that has the Gentiles in its purview, the introduction has Peter emphasize the privileges of the Jews in which all have now become participants. While the gospel was first preached to the Jews, still the Christ of God who was proclaimed is Lord of all (cf. Rom. 10:12). So in the conclusion the Jewish priority is stressed: it was the prophets of Israel who first announced Jesus. Yet this was only as one through whom every one who believes in him receives forgiveness of sins: the message was the universality of salvation by faith. The development of the discourse surrounding the central element parallels the early mission of Jesus with the mission that has been allotted him in the eschatological future. The earthly mission is described according to the familiar Gospel pattern, though for rhetorical effect the order is varied. We hear, in other words, of a ministry which began in Galilee after the baptism preached by John the Baptist, a ministry of the word accompanied by healing miracles and exorcisms manifesting the power of the Spirit of God and culminating in Jerusalem with Jesus' passion and death. Jesus, says Peter, was anointed by God with the Holy Spirit: the allusion, as in Acts 4:27 and Luke 4:18 (there a direct citation), is to Isa. 61:1, to the mission appointed the Servant of the Lord. So also in v. 36, the gospel or good news of peace proclaimed by Jesus is seen in relation to Isa. 52:7, the salvation made manifest to all mankind (cf. 52:10) through the ministry of this Servant. Luke is offering a Christian definition of the acceptation under which Jesus was recognized as Messiah, that is, the Anointed One. The eschatological mission of Jesus the Servant is to be by God's designation judge of both the living and the dead. "Ordained" is a favorite Lucan word (six times in Luke-Acts, elsewhere only twice in the New Testament), especially to refer to the salvific plan of God. It is also the Greek of Rom. 1:14, in part of what is thought to be a primitive Christian creedal formulation, to characterize the effect of the resurrection in constituting Christ Son of God in power. It is the resurrection, of course, which is the central assertion of this present catechesis. In keeping with its perspective as earliest preaching, however, it is to be noted that the resurrection here figures only as the act of God which has, so to speak, canceled out the ignominy of the crucifixion. The cross is not proclaimed as a salvific event in itself, but merely as the end of Jesus' earthly career.

Second Lesson: Col. 3:1–4. Greatly different is the perspective on the resurrection offered by our Second Lesson. Colossians is one of those writings which many scholars nowadays characterize as deutero-Pauline. That is to say, while they concede that its doctrine is basically Pauline, it represents a development of Paul's thought which the apostle himself never reached. Others, however, find nothing in the way of recognizing in Colossians (and Ephesians) simply the expression of another dimension of resurrection faith which Paul found it necessary to draw out and apply to the situation at hand. Certainly it is true that whereas in the "major" Pauline Epistles the resurrection of Christ is set forth as the basis of the hope of Christians in a future salvation and resurrection of their own (and in 1 Cor. 15, at least, Paul had to insist most vehemently on the futurity of the latter event), in Colossians (and Ephesians) Christians are regarded as already raised up with Christ.

The reason for this emphasis is to be found in the peculiar situation of the Colossians. The church at Colossae, in the Lycus Valley of Asia Minor, had not been founded personally by Paul, but it was one in which he took a deep interest. False teachers had arisen there disturbing the young church by preaching the necessity of certain ritual practices, dietary and ascetical observances, and a kind of Gnosticism based on supposed visions and superior knowledge of the proper approach to God. The Pauline answer to such pretensions was, as in Galatians 3—5, to insist on the all-sufficiency of faith in Christ, or the freedom with which Christ has made us free, and the life of the Spirit which is the only law for Christians. More radically than in Galatians, however, the position is stated that the Christian has not simply been declared free of earthly rules and powers but has effectively died to them by sharing in the death of Christ and being raised to heavenly life where such things have no meaning.

"Raised up with" Christ is a single word in the original text: "conresurrected" would be the term we would have to coin to convey the resonance adequately. The word has already appeared in 2:12 along with another, "buried with him in baptism," that is, "consepulchered" or something like. In the following v. 13 we read that in the resurrection of Jesus, God made Christians "alive together with him," that is to say again, "convivified." This is all part of the special vocabulary of Colossians-Ephesians, the use of "*syn*-words," the compounding of verbs or other words with the preposition *syn*, "with," in order to express with utmost vividness the total participation of the Christian in the salvific death, resurrection, and exaltation of Christ. It is, as has already been pointed out, a present participation. However, the customary Pauline eschatological perspective remains: only when Christ our life appears in the manifestation of his glory *will* we also appear with him in glory (here no *syn*-verb, v. 4).

The message of Colossians is not, therefore, of a present "mystical" union with the glorified Christ which would render superfluous any eschatological hope, which would make salvation such a present reality that the Christian could afford to remain aloof from mundane realities—such as the proper ordering in fraternal love of the body of believers which is the church. Such was, very nearly, the error of "realized eschatology" which Paul had to combat in his Letter to the Corinthians. The insistence here on present union with Christ is, as always in Pauline theology, entirely pragmatic. We must bear in mind the context, in which 3:1–4 appears as a conclusion; namely, a treatment of Christian freedom and of the consequences of Christian faith. The "things that are above" which Christians must seek are, in this context, opposed to "things that are on earth," and the latter are those ritual and other observances which the false teachers of Colossae were proposing as necessary to a full Christian life but from which, in fact, the reality of the Christ event has set us free. The things that are above, then, are heavenly things (where Christ is, seated at the right hand of God), but "heavenly" only in the sense that this is the Christ-revealed dimension under which the present realities of the Christian life are to be assessed and sought. Far from being an invitation to complacency in a salvation already assured, the exhortation is a summons to a continuing evaluation of and action in a present life made possible through God's grace revealed in Christ.

Gospel: John 20:1–18. The Johannine version of the resurrection story fairly bristles with exegetical difficulties, not only as regards its relationship to the synoptic parallels but also in its internal coherence and its connection with the rest of the Fourth Gospel. It might be thought, indeed, that the evangelist could have omitted a resurrection story entirely, in view of his portrayal of the crucifixion as already the beginning of Christ's glorification; however, it is obvious that the common Christian tradition to which he subscribed would allow him no such thing. It is impossible to ignore the fact that this part of the Gospel as well as many others bears unmistakable signs of redaction, of joining together of what were originally separate bits of tradition. We must be content with examining briefly the two episodes described in the text, which coincidentally feature the two preeminent elements in the early Christian witness to the resurrection, namely the empty tomb and the appearances of the Risen Lord.

The empty tomb was actually featured in the earliest tradition as an occasion rather than a motive for faith in the resurrection. It is, as seems obvious, a tradition that grew up in Jerusalem, and those scholars are doubtless correct who insist that it was taken into the tradition only secondarily, after the story of the appearances. (In 1 Cor. 15:3–7, where Paul cites primitive tradition about the resurrection, the empty tomb is probably not alluded to; but this point has been disputed.) As it figures in John's Gospel, the empty tomb is indeed a motive for belief, at least for "the disciple whom Jesus loved," that person who so often in the Gospel stands for the present Christian who lives by the faith witness of the church. The significance of the burial cloths seen both by him and by Simon Peter (without a mention of corresponding faith on Peter's part) is not entirely clear, but in some fashion what must have been meant is that they testified to no casual removal of a dead body from the tomb but to the resurrection of one who had discarded them. Neither is it clear what was the Scripture to which John refers, according to which "he must rise from the dead." Obviously, as in Luke 24:27, it is assumed that in the light of resurrection faith the Christian has access to a meaning of the OT (Hos. 6:2, let us say by way of example) that transcends its historical sense. It is to be noted that if the empty tomb had convincing force for the beloved disciple, though probably not for Peter (in keeping with Luke 24:11, according to which the disciples did not accept the testimony of the first witnesses to the empty tomb), it definitely plays no role in the faith of Mary Magdalene. She comes to the tomb while it is still dark: in John's Gospel, darkness signifies the unredeemed, unbelieving world prior to the manifestation of the Light which is Christ the Lord. She does not look on the burial cloths but only sees that the stone has been taken away from the tomb.

Only in John's Gospel is Mary Magdalene alone featured among the women who were the first witnesses to the empty tomb (cf. the synoptic parallels). She alone, too, figures in this story unique to John in which she becomes the first to experience an appearance of the resurrected Christ. That she should have failed at first to recognize the Lord is in keeping with other traditions (Luke 24:13–35, for example), which implies that in the passing from this life and death into the heavenly sphere of resurrected life, changes had taken place which could only be penetrated by the faith which the appearances evoked. That Mary recognizes Christ only in his calling her by name—the word which is proclaimed in the church—corresponds with the disciples of Luke 24:35 recognizing him in the breaking of the bread—the sacramental ministry of the church. "Do not [continue to] hold me" in 20:17 is not in conflict with 20:27, according to which the risen Christ bids Thomas to touch him. Jesus is telling Mary that his exaltation is not yet complete and must not be hindered: "I have not yet ascended to the Father." The Johannine concept of resurrection and return to heaven does not allow, as does the Lucan, for a relatively lengthy period of time between resurrection and ascension, but it does separate the two as distinct theological emphases. So also the early Christian liturgy celebrated the two events on one day without confounding their separate significance.

HOMILETICAL INTERPRETATION

Palm branches, crosses, and an empty tomb. It's an odd story we Christians believe. One surprise follows another. Holy Week seems to get out of hand. We lose control. Is that because in reality God is in control, though we find it hard to believe? It all looms in our memory now—a confusing collage of comedy and tragedy; Hosannas turned to "Crucify him!"; a quiet meal and an ugly scene on a hill. Somehow everything happens too fast.

And now Easter is upon us. All the weeks of penitent preparation have ended. From the dark of Lent we move into the light of Easter. From the dark of our sin and our poor attempts at repentance we stumble into the light of Christ's resurrection, rubbing our eyes, not quite sure we can believe what we see. Maybe that's because we only see what we believe—a slim faith yields little insight.

How unfortunate for many Christians that Easter exists only from the crack of Easter dawn to the dusk of Easter eve. At one time the church celebrated the resurrection every Sunday. A preacher speaking before others about doing a Lenten series was asked, "What do you do when Easter comes along?" He replied, "Oh, I usually interrupt my Lenten series for Easter." How can the central event of the church's life become more than a mere interruption?

First Lesson: Acts 10:34–43. Budding evangelists could take their cues from the scene in Acts. The models for evangelism here reveal a lot about conversion and the growth of the church. Peter, a dedicated Jew, is on his way to Cornelius's house. But it's more than a pastoral visit, more than an uninvited evangelist knocking at the door. Cornelius has asked for Peter. Like many gleeful secularists today, Cornelius is more religious than he knows, but more curious than the young-eyed ones seeking a new high from the latest guru. He is serious about his questioning. And so Peter, the dedicated Jew, is on his way to Cornelius's house. Where is the revival tent, the impersonal camera of the electronic church? No strains of "Just As I Am" in the background. This man whose whole environment has taught him to avoid Gentiles is now on his way to Cornelius's house— coming in person. Why? Because of a dream at lunchtime—a dream about food. The dream is a conversion experience in itself. The Jew has to be converted before the Gentile can be. The social context here prevents mere human initiative. On their own, Blacks and whites don't naturally integrate. Why is Peter on his way to Cornelius's house? Because *God* has sent him there. God shows no partiality. Why did Jesus rise from the grave? Because God *raised* him. That's what Peter preaches when he gets to Cornelius's house. He preaches that the crucifixion was not the final word. He preaches the transforming power of the risen Lord. In fact, he goes there because his own life has been transformed.

No doubt Cornelius will be there Easter Sunday. We've seen him before, sitting on a back pew. He stumbles up the steps. Bewildered, seeking something. Not quite sure what. Something about the words on the marquee caught his attention. Or is he still at home waiting . . . waiting for us to come and tell about the resurrection? Is that God nudging us out the study door, nudging us who call ourselves witnesses?

Second Lesson: Col. 3:1–4. "If you have been raised with Christ . . ." That's a big "if." But the author presumes it to be the case. Again a large presumption. For to be raised with Christ one has first to have died to the world—no small task. How easy it is to cling to the world. I look around my home and wonder what I would do without small pleasures that feed selfish desires. None of these is bad in itself. But as Christ calls us upward we find ourselves caught in a thicket, entangled. Somehow in him we have to die to these to live a new life.

That is, of course, what the resurrection calls us to—a new life. God not only takes the initiative with Christ, he takes the initiative with us as well. To talk about resurrection solely in terms of Jesus—risen from the dead—is to miss the point of God's activity here. Christ's dying and rising are related to our dying and rising. All of this "up and down movement" occurs *with* Christ.

So, if that is the case, we are to do certain things. Indicative usually leads to imperative in the gospel. This passage operates as a hinge between doctrinal statement and practical exhortation. What do we do? "Seek things above." "Consider things above." Shun things on earth. Sounds like a good way to avoid moral responsibility. Spend all your time contemplating angels and listening for the heavenly choir. Hardly. Our Lord was no romantic saint. He knew the kind of world we live in. He was earthy. Just read his parables. There's a difference between staring at the sky and looking at the world through resurrection eyes.

Gospel: John 20:1–18. One of the great challenges in preaching today is to confront a text that has scholars scratching their heads. If scholars scratch their heads, preachers should be throwing up their hands. In this text several traditions converge. Unraveling them exegetically is worth the trouble. What do we discover?

First, we find that we've overplayed the cemetery scene. How often we preach the empty tomb as the sole message of the resurrection. But here the empty tomb plays a small role. It gives no message on its own, only mystery. If the empty tomb were all we had on which to base our faith, then ours would be a religion of the cemetery. Our story would start in a graveyard. And likely end there, too. You can almost see the gray mist of an English werewolf movie. As it stands, all we have is a rolled-back stone, a woman, and the men running about, fumbling with robes trying to figure what's happened. Only the "other" disciple gets the picture, and he has gotten the picture first throughout John's Gospel. Ours is not a religion of the cemetery but a religion of the risen Lord.

This brings us to the second point. Understanding comes only with "recognition" of the risen Lord. And here seeing isn't always believing. In this case *hearing* may be believing. Weeping Mary can't make him out through her tears. The question "Why are you weeping?" is more a theological point than pastoral care. John's Jesus knew all along that he was supposed to die. There's no reason to weep, especially not now. She sees him but does not see really. Not until he calls her name. You know what it's like to hear an unmistakable voice; familiar, but with a new ring to it. To hear that voice call *your* name makes all the difference. Then you can say, "I have seen the Lord."

Easter Evening or
Easter Monday

Lutheran	Roman Catholic	Episcopal
Dan. 12:1c–3 or Jon. 2:2–9	Acts 2:14, 22–32	Acts 5:29a, 30–32 or Dan. 12.1–3
1 Cor. 5:6–8		1 Cor. 5:6b–8 or Acts 5:29a, 30–32
Luke 24:13–49	Matt. 28:8–15	Luke 24:13–35

EXEGESIS

First Lesson: Acts 2:14, 22–32. The First Lesson for today as well as for Easter 2 is concerned with what Acts represents as an important sequel to the event of Pentecost, "the baptism of the church." It is the first of the discourses attributed to Peter, a Jewish catechesis ("men of Judea and all who dwell in Jerusalem," "men of Israel") as opposed to the gentile catechesis of Acts 10:34–43. Pentecost was of course a Jewish festival, the Feast of Weeks, celebrated fifty days after the Passover. Originally a feast of the wheat harvest, by NT times Pentecost had come to be celebrated in commemoration of the giving of the law at Mount Sinai, even as Passover commemorated the Exodus from Egypt. Furthermore, rabbinic tradition had speculated that at Sinai the law had been proclaimed "in all the languages of the earth" (which the rabbis calculated at seventy) as a kind of reversal of the confusion of tongues that had taken place at Babel. Something of this sort of symbolism seems to lie behind the account of the first Christian Pentecost as Acts tells it. The manifestation of the Spirit in wind and fire (cf. Exod. 19:16–20) with the accompanying glossolalia is interpreted by Peter as the enactment of a new covenant typified by the old, and in vv. 17–21 he cites Joel 2:28–32 (freely and according to the Greek text of the OT) as being fulfilled in this coming of the messianic age. The catechesis then follows: Jesus is the Messiah prophesied for this messianic age.

The catechesis may be outlined as follows: (1) Jesus of Nazareth was a man attested by God with wonders and signs, as the Jews of Palestine know full well (v. 22). This assertion is an epitome of the gospel story. (2) The crucifixion (again, the scandal of the cross: cf. Matt. 16:21–23) is in no wise proof that Jesus failed in his messianic mission, for *(a)* it was foreseen by God and included in his providential plan, *(b)* it is evidence only of human malice, Jewish and gentile alike, and *(c)* it has been canceled out by the resurrection (vv. 23–24). (3) That Christ has been resurrected in fulfillment of prophecy is the subject of a lengthy development (vv. 25–32). Finally, (4) Christ now reigns in heaven as Lord and Christ, as is proved by this recent manifestation of the Spirit (vv. 33–36). These final verses, which are not assigned to this day's reading by the lectionary, are nevertheless integral to the discourse. In this catechesis to the Jews, then, there is a stress on prophecy, on assigning guilt for the judicial murder of a man of God, on the resurrection as having nullified the scandal of the cross, and (in 4) on the resurrection as the font of the Spirit-life of the church.

The argument (in 3) by which Peter is made to portray the resurrection as the fulfillment of prophecy is a good example of early Christian rereading of the OT in the light of NT events. It makes use of the old Greek translation of Psalm 16: despite efforts to show the contrary, it is extremely doubtful that the original Hebrew can be made to sustain the sense ascribed to this text in vv. 25–28. It also rests on assumptions which would have been shared by a Jewish audience of the time: that David was author of the Psalms, that he was a prophet who foresaw the future, that the historical meaning of Scripture is secondary to its values for spiritual accommodation, among others. These suppositions accepted, the argument is that David the prophet, who knew that he was to be ancestor of the Messiah (Ps. 132:11), must have been speaking of this Messiah rather than of himself in the first person pronouns of Ps. 16:8–11. For while there has never been any doubt that David died and was buried in the normal way, with his body returning to its elements, the disciples are witness to the resurrection of Jesus, David's descendant. Such exegetical processes, we may be sure, were those regularly employed in the new understanding of prophecy to which the church felt itself guided by the Spirit (see Acts 8:32–35, for example).

Second Lesson: 1 Cor. 5:6–8. The church at Corinth was founded by Paul (Acts 18:1–17) and forever after continued to vex him with its numerous excesses, second thoughts, and backslidings. In 1 Corinthians Paul shrewdly analyzed the root of the problems of this young church as its dominant false pride (the "boasting" of 1 Cor. 5:6) which led it into snobbery of various kinds, class distinctions, playing apostolic authorities off each other, complacency in a supposedly superior understanding of "true" Christianity, and all the rest. He is at pains throughout to ridicule the Corinthians' pretensions none too gently, and in 5:1–5 he has just brought up an example of disorder among them of such magnitude that it should shake their confidence in themselves once and for all. In vv. 6–8 he appends an exhortation phrased in language that could have come very naturally to him in its essential Jewishness.

Before celebrating the Passover, the Feast of Unleavened Bread, every bit of leavening material had to be removed from Jewish homes, and careful search had to be made to get rid of every trace of it lest its well-known power for contagion should corrupt the new dough for the feast. The Corinthians are being compared to this new dough, which should be dedicated to the sincerity and truth of a new Christian Passover. The new life has been inaugurated by the sacrificial death of Christ, here likened to the slaying of the Passover lamb which at that time was integral to the festival. The danger is that they can be contaminated by the old leaven, the old ways of malice and evil concretely represented by the incestuous man of v. 1. Paul's exhortation has a threefold purpose, therefore: It is an injunction for them to set their house in order by exercising discipline over unruly members. It is a warning against the danger of evil associations. And it is, deep down, a rebuke of Corinthian arrogance, which has tolerated this scandal while pretending to have its eye directed toward the higher things of religion.

Gospel: Matt. 28:8–15. The Gospel passage for today is an extract from a distinctively Matthean version of the resurrection story. That story falls into three natural divisions: the witnesses to the empty tomb according to Matthew (vv. 1–10); a Jerusalemite appendix to the tradition which is peculiar to the First Gospel (vv. 11–15); and the commissioning of the disciples by the resurrected Christ (vv. 16–20). The lectionary has selected part of the first and all of the second of these divisions to make up its reading.

We begin with the first witnesses to the empty tomb, who in Matthew are Mary Magdalene and "the other Mary" (presumably the mother of James and Joseph mentioned in 27:56), hastening with fear and joy to tell the disciples of the event. The picture contrasts strangely with that of Mark 16:7–8, where the women are all-fearful and, at first at least, say nothing to anyone, even though they have been instructed to report to the disciples. The development in vv. 9–10 is somewhat strange and jars a bit in context. Some have suggested that this is a Matthean version of the appearance of the risen Christ to Mary Magdalene recorded in John 20:11–18. In the Matthean context what is important is the instruction that the disciples are to go to Galilee, for in Matthew's Gospel, unlike those of Luke and John, it is in Galilee rather than Judea that the Jesus story has its conclusion, even as there it began.

The episode of vv. 11–15, however, certainly represents a Jerusalem tradition, a complement to the tradition of the empty tomb which obviously originated there. "The guard" are, in Matthew's mind, the Roman soldiers whom the Jewish leadership had requested of Pilate to insure the tomb of Jesus against any tampering on the part of his disciples (27:64–66) and who were also, in their own way, witnesses to the empty tomb (28:2–4). Here, like the mercenaries they were, they are represented as testifying, for pay, to the false story that the dead body of Jesus had been stolen away by his disciples, to account for the empty tomb. This narrative tells us a number of things. First of all, it attests to what was undoubtedly a part of Jewish polemics against Christian resurrection faith in the early days of the church: in his *Dialogue with Trypho* written toward the middle of the second century, the church father Justin Martyr records that this tale of tomb robbery was still current among the Jews. Secondly, it fits into a pattern of hostility to official Judaism which is a distinct characteristic of the First Gospel, undoubtedly reflecting a milieu of the Matthean church (Syria?) in which church and synagogue were in daily conflict on many issues. And finally, perhaps most importantly, it underscores the fact that within the NT the phenomenon of the empty tomb was in fact an ambiguous sign subject to contradictory interpretations.

HOMILETICAL INTERPRETATION

This morning we arrived at the tomb and began to discover that our Lord has risen, he has risen indeed. If the empty tomb was not persuasive, our Lord's voice was. Our dying and rising with him became more real as we began to recognize who he was and what he had done. Our witnessing to this fact sends us into places that we would not normally enter. This evening we continue to ponder the power of Christ's resurrection and even more the challenges it presents for us in our missionary and moral responsibilities as Christians.

First Lesson: Acts 2:14, 22–32. If this morning's passage about Peter presented an odd prototype for evangelism, this one is even more unusual. Here the Jews have gathered for the Feast of Weeks, which likely means that Jews from different places have now settled in Jerusalem. They are interrupted by some minor disturbance. Wind and fire (sure signs of the Spirit) appear. Tongues-speaking causes a din of chatter. But suddenly they could all understand, as if everyone had put on headphones at the United Nations. The babble made sense. The curse of Babel was reversed. The only explanation was, "They're drunk." Up pops Peter, the impetuous one—ready with an explanation and a gospel to preach. "They can't be drunk—it's only nine in the morning. But while I have your attention, let me tell you about Jesus Christ." And off he goes. A new evangelistic technique—or maybe very old. Something surprising happens, and the apostle uses it as an occasion for conversion. But a caution against seeing these events too literally. The point is that God surprises us with his intervention. It is his action that converts and moves a community. How can we employ those surprises as opportunities to witness?

Notice the shift in the lectionary choices from the gentile mission to the Jewish mission. We've established the universal character of our mission on Easter morning. That is what our God is up to. Now we concentrate on the difficult mission to the Jews. Peter's sermon directly addresses them. "Men of Israel, hear these words." He pulls no punches. The cross is a scandal, to be sure. ("But we preach Christ crucified, a stumbling block to Jews," 1 Cor. 1:23a.) But it is not the end of God's work. The God of Abraham, Isaac, and Jacob has a hand in this. Surprise. He raised Jesus up. Not only that, David, our hero, talked about him. Take another look at Psalm 16. Quoting David with respect in this manner was like someone citing Lee to an audience of Southerners. Finally, God may take the initiative in this action, but he expects us to move with it. "And of that we are all witnesses" suggests that no letters are written in the sky. Someone has to witness. That is God's way. It hints at the message of the Gospel lesson.

Second Lesson: 1 Cor. 5:6–8. Most good theology arises out of conflicts. Whether it be Augustine attacking the Manichaeans, the Donatists, and the Pelagians, or Paul taking on Gnostic perfectionists, the refining that occurs usually sharpens our faith. Here Paul moves from scandal to theology. He attacks immoral actions and turns church discipline into doctrine. (Of course, church discipline not grounded in doctrine usually lapses into secular conflict management—not bad in itself but limited.) The problem here is arrogance. In the name of Christian freedom the Corinthians were accepting immorality because of an unwarranted pride. Paul moves to a homely example that his hearers would understand.

Funny thing about leaven. It spreads. A little bit goes a long way. What's the point? The immoral behavior of one person can infect a whole group. Description then turns to prescription. Cleanse out the old leaven. Be in church practice what you already know in belief. Live the Christian life that you said you would when you took the vows to join the church. And here is where the theology comes in. As in the Passover, Christ was sacrificed. This is the reason that for a long time Easter was called the Pascha or Christian Passover. Paul's point here is very simple. If you are going to partake of the Lord's Supper, then do it as if you mean to live it. Otherwise your action is blasphemous.

Combine the Colossians passage for this morning with this passage and you see the implications of the resurrection in the two sacraments of Baptism and Eucharist. The implications are not only sacramental but moral. What Jesus lived for continues as we grow in the Christian faith and carry on his work in the world.

Gospel: Matt. 28:8–15. Matthew attacks the chief priests for attempting to stifle the story about Christ's resurrection. How ridiculous and how impossible to try to hide the fact of his rising. Trying to hide the fact of the resurrection is like trying to hold back the coming dawn. God won't allow it. Once we "catch sight" of him, nothing will hold back our joy.

This story is about more than tomb thievery and a group of people conjuring explanations for a body's absence. It's about an unsuccessful attempt to keep the disciples' explanation from seeing light of day. But to dwell on this element would miss the point. Apparently Matthew's audience did dwell on it. Matthew's audience is arrogant (here arrogance is not the same as in the Second Lesson and should not be turned into a topical sermon on arrogance using the two passages). They assume that the resurrection is a historical fact. And if it is a fact, why preach it? All should be able to see its historicity. The fact is, all don't see it; so we have to preach it. Our risen Lord interrupts us in our running and rushing about to give us instructions. "Go and tell my brethren to go to Galilee, and there they will see me." We are called to be witnesses to the resurrection. Can we? Will we? If we aren't witnesses, no one has to stifle the story; we have done it ourselves.

The Second Sunday of Easter

Lutheran	Roman Catholic	Episcopal	Pres/UCC/Chr	Meth/COCU
Acts 2:14a, 22–32	Acts 2:42–47	Acts 2:14a, 22–32 or Gen. 8:6–16; 9:8–16	Acts 2:42–47	Acts 2:14a, 22–32 or Gen. 8:6–16; 9:8–16
1 Pet. 1:3–9	1 Pet. 1:3–9	1 Pet. 1:3–9 or Acts 2:14a, 22–32	1 Pet. 1:3–9	1 Pet. 1:3–9
John 20:19–31	John 20:19–31	John 20:19–31	John 20:19–31	John 20:19–31

EXEGESIS

First Lesson: Acts 2:14a, 22–32. See the exegesis for the First Lesson for Easter Evening or Easter Monday.

Second Lesson: 1 Pet. 1:3–9. The First Epistle of Peter is a treasury of early Christian thought remarkably like Paul's (some would say by direct dependence on the Pauline literature) and also of independent apostolic traditions of obvious antiquity. Traditionally the work of Peter the apostle (1:1) written by him at Rome (5:13, "Babylon"), it contains in any case ample intrinsic credentials to stand as one of the most important of the works of the NT, at the very heart of the Christian gospel, as Martin Luther recognized. It is a highly ecclesiastical work: one view of it, not entirely abandoned by scholars, is that at its background lies a baptismal liturgy which is systematically incorporated or paraphrased. Written to gentile Christians of Asia Minor (1:1), it is a work of consolation and encouragement (5:12) to a church of the "second generation" of Christianity (1:8) suffering persecution or at least liable to persecution because of the Christian profession.

The lesson for today is the beginning of a thanksgiving of hymnic quality which, in the Pauline mode (cf. 1 Cor. 1:4–9), follows the epistolary salutation. The perspective is also Pauline: the epistle is composed from the standpoint of the early Christian eschatological expectation. Through the resurrection Christians have been born again, in hope of an inheritance. The inheritance is unfailing and sure, but it is still kept in heaven. The faith of Christians is toward a salvation which is to be revealed in the last time. It is possible that rival claimants to a way of salvation—the here-and-now salvation professed by the mystery religions of Asia Minor from which these Christians had emerged and which continued to dominate the culture in which they lived—were the reason for this stress on future eschatology and at the same time caused the Christians' fear of persecution. What is very much present, however, and what constitutes the motivation for this thanksgiving, is the faith, love, and joy which unites Christians with their Lord and with one another. These await fulfillment but not improvement in the future. The trials which are the Christian destiny (4:12–13; cf. Luke 22:28) are sent not to purify faith but to prove its genuineness, even as gold, a far less precious commodity, is tested by fire (v. 7).

Gospel: John 20:19–31. Today we see the conclusion of the Johannine resurrection story begun on Easter Sunday together with what was, in all probability, the original ending of John's Gospel itself, in which the overall purpose of the Gospel is clearly set forth. Several exegetical points call for remark; many others unfortunately cannot be noted here.

First of all, the appearance of the risen Lord to the disciples is obviously intended by the evangelist to highlight the commission given them for the forgiveness of sins. The "peace" with which Jesus greets the disciples is no ordinary conventional greeting. It is the fulfillment of the promise made in the Last Supper discourse (14:25–29), there also bound up with the giving of the Holy Spirit, the promise of one who already spoke as the glorified Lord of the church (13:31–32). The solemn bestowal of the Spirit under these circumstances confirms that in this section we have the Johannine Pentecost, the redemptive mission communicated to the church: "As the Father has sent me, even so I send you." The judicial language in which the power over sins is announced reminds us of Matt. 16:19 and 18:18. The church is constituted not merely as a body of believers each of whom has individually received forgiveness of sins in faith and baptism but as a governed organism in which the power of forgiveness is actively administered through the ministry of word and sacrament.

The episode of "doubting Thomas" allows John to make a final statement of what he understands to be the nature of true faith. In the Johannine sense Thomas is doubly unbelieving, first because he refuses to accept the apostolic word and secondly because he demands some physical wonder as the price of his belief. Miracles, for John, are a shaky basis on which to build faith. Nevertheless, he is brought by the presence of Christ (and probably without the actual touching of his body which he had first required) to the most explicit christological affirmation of the entire NT. It is this divine Lord of Thomas's profession who is the subject of the church's preaching, and through hearing this word comes true faith (v. 29).

Hence John's conclusion in vv. 30–31. The "signs" which Jesus worked were indeed, as in the synoptic Gospels, his miraculous deeds. Yet they are more than this. In the Gospel of John miracles are deprecated more than once as a ground for faith (see 4:48, for example); but in any case Jesus' miracles were witnessed by only a comparative few at a time remote from the readers of the Fourth Gospel, who believe without having seen. The signs that have been written in this Gospel, therefore, are the enduring evidences for Christ's divine sonship as they are manifest in the church which does his works and works that are greater than his works because of his glorification (14:12). The preaching and ministry of the church perpetuate his signs, perceptible only to the eye of faith, which point the way to everlasting life.

HOMILETICAL INTERPRETATION

It should be apparent by now that last Sunday was the beginning of something big. We celebrated the fact of our Lord's resurrection and the consequences of his rising for our own Christian lives. Easter Sunday is not the end of Lent and the church year but the commencement of new life for us and the church. The story gets richer week by week, not only in the Christian year but in the years of our lives. Why then has this Sunday been called Low Sunday in England? Why has it seemed to be Lowest Sunday in America? We should continue the joy that began a week ago when we sang, "Jesus Christ is risen today, Alleluia!"

There are several themes working in today's passages. One that is traditional for this Sunday is Christ's demonstration of his hands and feet. The connection between crucifixion and resurrection is made clear so that no one misunderstands. Another theme is the giving of the Spirit. Pentecost is in the background in the First Lesson and the Gospel, but be careful about trying to harmonize them too much. This theme leads directly to the next. The promise of the Spirit attends the commissioning of the disciples. Without the Spirit they would be only traveling salesmen peddling a human message about a dead savior. The final theme is believing without seeing.

First Lesson: Acts 2:14a, 22–32. We've already established that the background for this passage is the Lucan account of Pentecost. Peter's speech to the multitude (2:6) follows the descent of the Holy Spirit upon the company of believers, which Jesus promised at the time of his ascension (1:8). Here the Spirit and the commission to be witnesses come together. Peter has obviously taken the commission seriously. He has surely been empowered to speak. Peter, who thrice denied his Lord and cowered in the shadows when asked about him, now speaks with boldness: "Men of Israel, hear these words." Why the new courage? Why this turnaround, this forthrightness which even went beyond Peter's precrucifixion statements? It must be the Spirit. So the Spirit comes and Peter speaks. Again we see the transforming power of our risen Lord.

As we noted last week, Peter concentrates on the crucifixion. To avoid it would be an oversight of no small dimension. It was part of God's plan that Christ be "delivered up" and "crucified." And yet how often we do overlook the cross. It's difficult even now to look at a crucifix for very long. How often we jump from hosannas to Easter joy and look clean past the cross. For years the church celebrated Good Friday and Easter as one event. Now we have split them in two, and many churches simply forget Good Friday. Little wonder. It spells Christ's suffering and our suffering as well. We know enough about suffering. Don't talk to us of suffering. But without the cross the empty tomb is just another grave. Christ has broken the shackles of death. God has raised him up. Not until the cross becomes for us truly a scandal (our God defeated and rejected) will the resurrection have any meaning. Until we see all our hopes dashed and destroyed (even if partly by our own hands), the Easter hymns will remain only nice songs with a few good tunes. We have to be down before we know what it is to be lifted up.

Second Lesson: 1 Pet. 1:3–9. Certainly the Christians in Asia Minor knew what it was to be down. Their suffering was real. Their persecution tried what little faith they had. After all, they had never seen Jesus. They had no stories to swap about experiences with the Lord. Their faith was secondhand, or so they thought. The absence of Christ makes it tough to believe. We know that. It's especially difficult to believe in "an inheritance which is imperishable, undefiled, and unfading, kept in heaven for you." Sounds like a lifetime layaway plan or an eternal lifetime guarantee. Good for the future, like "getting a piece of the rock"; but what about now? Now we work out our salvation here on earth. We try everything, living in the "me generation." It's a thrill a minute "doing it my way." Have a belt, get a fix—anything to dull the pain. Some get high, some low. But everything turns sour all too soon. Maybe something eschatological would be more lasting.

Here is the message that these Christians needed to hear. Rejoice about your glorious inheritance in Christ. God knows we've rejoiced about much less. All of it fades. Yes, God knows. So we believe in a man who suffered as we do. Even more, he suffered for me. Now he suffers with us. But sooner or later we have to get beyond the suffering. Oh, we never escape it—just don't set up camp in it. Some of us suffer so much that we never get beyond Good Friday. It's the reverse of the earlier problem. Some of us never get to Easter. Then the suffering becomes unbearable. When someone dies, all we hear is Good Friday silence. Certainly our Lord "pitched his tent" among us. But he never "pitches tent" in the empty tomb. He is out and about and at the right hand of God. And because he is, we have hope. We can rejoice in the midst of suffering because of our hope in Christ Jesus. No wonder this passage sounds like a hymn (probably baptismal). It makes you want to sing.

Gospel: John 20:19–31. Last week we poked around the empty tomb; this week we move out of the cemetery because Christ has moved out. This week Christ comes to us. One wonders how Hollywood would handle these scenes. Ghosts, no doubt, floating about. But John would not be interested. In fact, there's a move here from the spiritual to a more physical presence. Again, the point is not that it makes for a good story or that we're interested in what form bodies take after death, but that Jesus is making the tie between his crucifixion and his resurrection. To see them separately is to miss the point. "See my hands and side." William Temple believed that Christ's wounds were his credentials to all suffering people. So our risen Lord stands before us as the one who died on the cross. The thought is dizzying but true. Not only that, he greets us with more than a "Hello, how are you doing?" The "Peace be with you" here relates to the Spirit promised by Christ. The Spirit is given in his breath. And in one breath the *ruach* that brought Adam to his feet and brought Judah (in Ezekiel's vision) together with a rattle and a clatter sent the disciples on the road with a gospel to preach. That same *pneuma* changes lives today and turns seminary chatter into preaching for the church. It turns disciples into apostles. Followers suddenly become leaders. Their schooling is over now. Now they become teachers. It's tough to be pushed out on your own. Some of us would like to stay in school all our lives. We feel safe and comfortable there. But Christ sends us out. He pushes us out the door. All of this is true except in John. In John disciples remain disciples so we are on our own but not alone. Christ is still our teacher and the Spirit becomes our companion—the Paraclete.

Now there's another matter in this passage. What to do with poor Thomas, the much-maligned disciple. Doubting Thomas was not so slow, not so obstinate. He simply wanted some answers. He had missed the sunrise service and the first appearance. And being the true skeptic that he was (the Twin, "two-minded, doubting") he wanted some proof. If Cornelius was in church last Sunday, Thomas is here today. He heard the roar, the singing, and he's here to find out what all the fuss is about. We shouldn't be too hard on Thomas. He speaks our lines here. Are there not times we want a sign? We want to believe in God. If only he would show us a sign. The fact is, he doesn't need to. He already has, many times over, especially in Christ. Once that struck Thomas, his searching doubt turned to a deep faith. Disbelief turned to belief. His "My Lord and my God" (somewhere between vocative and indicative) is unmatched in the NT. The greatest skeptic becomes the greatest believer. And what is the message for us? Again, seeing isn't always believing. Simple, and yet not so simple.

The Third Sunday of Easter

Lutheran	Roman Catholic	Episcopal	Pres/UCC/Chr	Meth/COCU
Acts 2:14a, 36–47	Acts 2:14, 22–28	Acts 2:14a, 36–47 or Isa. 43:1–12	Acts 2:22–28	Acts 2:14a, 36–47 or Isa. 43:1–12
1 Pet. 1:17–21	1 Pet. 1:17–21	1 Pet. 1:17–23 or Acts 2:14a, 36–47	1 Pet. 1:17–21	1 Pet. 1:17–23
Luke 24:13–35	Luke 24:13–35	Luke 24:13–35	Luke 24:13–35	Luke 24:13–35

EXEGESIS

First Lesson: Acts 2:14a, 36–47. The passage from Acts first gives the climax of the Petrine discourse we have seen the past two weeks, then continues with two narrative sections on the early life of the Jerusalem church.

Just as in the christological hymn of Phil. 2:6–11, the culmination of Acts 2:22–36 is reached in the assertion that by the resurrection God has constituted Jesus our Lord (cf. Rom. 1:4). More precisely, he has so constituted him by an act of exaltation (cf. v. 33): Luke, unlike John, sees resurrection and exaltation as separate events temporally as well as specifically. "Lord" is without doubt the supreme title bestowed by the earliest Christianity on the glorified Redeemer. Whether it was adopted primarily, as some think, through imitation of the OT usage in reference to the God of Israel or was simply taken from among the titles common in the contemporary world to refer to divine beings, it was the designation probably best suited to identify for both Jews and Gentiles what Christians believed about their crucified Master. "Christ" was no mere translation of a parochial term for the Jewish Messiah but had become the designation of a divinely designated universal Savior.

The first major conversion in the Jewish church occurs in response to the Pentecost sermon. Baptism "in the name" of Jesus Christ is the common early designation of Christian Baptism (for there were other baptismal rites, both Jewish and gentile); see 8:16; 10:48; 19:5; 22:16; also 1 Cor. 6:11. This Baptism is "for the forgiveness of your sins," the effect of the redemption which God has worked through Christ (cf. 5:31 and 13:38), and in order that "you shall receive the gift of the Holy Spirit." The gift of the Holy Spirit *is* the Holy Spirit: the genitive is "epexegetical." Here is probably not meant the extraordinary manifestation of the Spirit just witnessed at Pentecost, though this will occur again in Acts in significant circumstances and sometimes accompanies Baptism (cf. 19:5–6). Rather, the gift of the Spirit is the fulfillment of "the promise" (v. 39; cf. v. 33) made to "your children and all that are far off," that is, to both Jew and Gentile (cf. Isa. 57:9; Eph. 2:13–17): even in this Jewish proclamation, redemption is the working of God's power for universal salvation. And as a matter of fact, those who now receive Baptism manifest no charismatic effects as a result but enter into the normal and ordered life of the church: adherence to the apostles' teaching, fellowship, the breaking of the bread, and the prayers.

Vv. 43–47, like 4:32–35, are part of an idealized portrait of early Christianity in Jerusalem, a narrative source that has probably been only partially preserved and in which there has been some rearrangement of material. The passage is nevertheless integral to the Christology and ecclesiology of Acts. Christ's presence is perpetuated in the persons of the apostles, and the communal charity and fellowship of the believers is eloquent testimony to everyone of the Holy Spirit that has come upon them.

Second Lesson: 1 Pet. 1:17-21. The passage begins on a cautionary note, but the emphasis speedily shifts to the positive as the ground for Christian hope and confidence are displayed. In the exile of this life all must be properly fearful of the consequences of their every deed, conscious of their accountability to an utterly just judge; yet the fact that they can call upon the judge as Father is already cause for hope, since he is their Father only in virtue of the redemptive work of Christ the Lord (v. 2) of which they have been made the recipients. This redemptive work has been effected not with perishable gold or silver but with the precious blood of Christ. What is in view in this exhortation to Gentiles is the process which was open to slaves by which they could legally accumulate enough personal wealth to ransom themselves from their masters and thus obtain freedom. In this case, however, freedom has been achieved through the death of one who is likened to a lamb without blemish or spot, that is, a perfect and adequate sacrifice. As in 1 Cor. 5:7, the reference is to the Passover lamb. This sacrifice has effected redemption from no mere temporary slavery but from an old way of life entirely meaningless and self-destructive. (The "vain" or "futile" of v. 18 is the term the OT applies to what is pernicious and deceptive, such as the gods of the Gentiles.) The confident hope of Christians rests, therefore, on a faith grounded on a recognition of the eternal plan of God now made manifest in the resurrection and exaltation of Christ.

Gospel: Luke 24:13-35. We have had occasion to mention this Gospel passage earlier in connection with others of this season. Luke alone of the canonical Gospels confines the appearances of the risen Christ to Jerusalem or its environs without any advertence to a return of the disciples to Galilee. In part this procedure is due to the artistic structure which the evangelist has imposed on his Gospel (and Acts), whereby Jerusalem must be both the beginning and the end of the first part of his work (whereas Jerusalem will be the beginning and Rome the end of the second part). The story of the disciples on the way to Emmaus is an exclusively Lucan account of postresurrection occurrences, and there is no doubt that it must be interpreted in keeping with Luke's particular theological purposes. Attempts to determine what is the "center" of Lucan theology, especially as set forth in the Gospel, have been many in the past and continue so in the present, without too much agreement among the scholars. We adopt here a position which would probably satisfy most as being general enough not to prejudge the significance of specific details while at the same time it captures the essential of what Luke has tried to do with his use of the gospel form. That is to say, Luke's is first and foremost an ecclesiastical Gospel, a Gospel which he has intended to be read with the day-by-day needs and instruction of the church in mind (note the introduction to the Gospel, especially 1:4). To this end he has "actualized" much of the Gospel content which he shares with the other evangelists (note for example 3:10–14, where he has introduced a little catechism pertaining to various categories of people in answer to the question of what they must do to show forth "fruits that befit repentance"). We believe that he has done no less in the material that is proper to his Gospel, and in this light we understand the function of the story of 24:13–35.

The day of the resurrection, two disciples who have received the women's witness to the empty tomb (vv. 22–24) but have remained unimpressed by this ambiguous testimony are overtaken on the way to Emmaus by a risen Christ whom they do not recognize. This initial failure to recognize the resurrected Lord on the part of those who had known him in earthly life is a common theme of Luke and John (John 20:14 and 21:4) and perhaps also Matthew (cf. Matt. 28:17). What is needed in every case is a word or sign before recognition takes place. Here there are both word and sign. First, after the disciples have delivered themselves of a fairly superficial accounting of "the things that have happened in these days concerning Jesus of Nazareth"— the sort of accounting that might have been made by any nonbeliever of moderate good will—Jesus interprets the Scriptures to them concerning the death and glorification of the Christ. Doubtless we are supposed to think of an interpretation such as that contained in the sermon of Acts 2:22–36. Even this word, however, though it is later recalled as a necessary complement (v. 32), does not effect total recognition. This comes finally only "in the breaking of the bread" in a rite evoking the language of Luke 22:19 and Acts 2:42, a sign which Luke could expect his readers to understand as an allusion to the Eucharist.

Only one further point need be made, from the perspective of Luke's ecclesiastical Gospel. We have seen above how in the Acts the apostles are represented as perpetuating the work of Christ, as being the *alteri christi* of the existing church. It was certainly in the ministry of apostolic missioners, and even or especially perhaps of itinerant missioners like Paul, that the truth and meaning of Jesus Christ was revealed in word and sacrament.

HOMILETICAL INTERPRETATION

This week's passages cover a wide spectrum of images and ideas. A simple summary would be: an ideal church, a reminder, and an unlikely stranger on the road. This, however, is not an outline for a three-point sermon. Actually there is more going on here. But there always is in Scripture, isn't there? In these passages we find a continued emphasis on the death of Christ and the meaning of his atoning sacrifice on the cross. We find also a highly sacramental emphasis. Last week hinted at Baptism; this week splashes into it. The disciples, whom Jesus called when they were knee-deep in nets, have three thousand others waist-deep in repentance. In addition, Eucharist is highlighted in the passages from Luke and Acts. The tandem experiences of recognition and conversion receive fuller examination. The Second Lesson looks at what to do once you have repented—how to avoid complacency. Finally, we begin to see in the Easter season a gradual movement from Christ's body (crucified and resurrected) to the body of Christ—the church.

First Lesson: Acts 2:14a, 36–47. Ever thought about starting your own religious group? There are lots of new ones popping up these days. How would you go about it? Read a book on new parish development? Maybe you would call together a committee to discuss the problem and establish ad hoc committees to take on certain tasks—a building committee, a budget committee, and of course an evangelism committee—not necessarily in that order.

Peter's way would likely have been rejected. It's certainly not an orderly way to start a church. What do we see here? Three thousand lined up by the river. The whole scene has the ethos of an old-time revival, the aura of the great awakenings in American history. Why do you suppose it worked? Perhaps it worked because it wasn't Peter's way at all, but God's.

The message about Christ's death and resurrection had finally begun to sink in, and there is almost a crack in their voices when they ask Peter, "What shall we do?" Peter's answer is not "Set up some committee" or "Let's raise some money" but "Repent, and be baptized." The retort must have been as unexpected as Jesus' "Repent or perish" in Luke 13. But some of them did repent, and what follows describes in brief the marks of the church. They taught, which probably means both teaching and preaching (both edification and evangelism). They shared a common life in *koinonia*. Here they cared for each other in all ways. They broke bread together, which signals a eucharistic meal, if only implicitly. Finally, they prayed together. Even as in marriage, a community that prays together stays together. There's another word—"they" didn't add to their number daily; the Lord did. That word is both a challenge and a liberation. We should help the Lord add to our number but not feel that it is totally our responsibility. It may also say something about church growth. We can always pad our rolls, but does the Lord want only packed pews on Sunday? He doesn't want empty pews. But he "added to their number . . . those who were being saved." The fact is, almost anybody can fill a church. We should take on the task of evangelism while all the time examining our motives and expectations and those of the ones coming. It is the risen Lord who transforms persons and adds to our number.

Not only do we see here an odd way to start a church, but the picture of its beginning seems too neat. Everybody seems too happy. Of course, we know that it doesn't stay this pleasant. Paul's Letters attest to that. And it hasn't been that way since. Just read church history, any period. Perhaps Luke is describing the ideal church, the way it should be, the best it can become, only with the help of God's Spirit. Seen in that light, it makes a pretty good model for all of us—that is, those of us who call ourselves Christians.

Second Lesson: 1 Pet. 1:17–21. This passage moves from command to theology rather than the other way around. Those addressed have probably been recently baptized, or received into the fellowship of the church. It's the kind of message that could have been used with the newly baptized in the Acts 2 account. It's the kind of message we need to hear, no matter how long ago we joined the church.

The whole passage (especially the beginning) sounds remarkably like a good old-fashioned sermon against backsliding. The only difference is that here there is not a heavy concentration on sin. The balance of the passage is not law but gospel. There is no sentence-by-sentence description of where we have fallen short with a prescription for what we "ought" to do. Only a small but poignant warning. But the warning is seen against the backdrop of Christ's atoning death and resurrection. I highlight this fact, because it would be easy to preach the passage as only a warning or a threat.

Having said that, I point out that the threat *is* real because we still live "in exile." Our fear should be real since God our loving Father is also our judge. Certainly those in Acts 2 understood. "And fear came upon every soul," we are told. How many in our churches really fear God these days? For most, God has become simply a long-lost friend, the friend they once had. Just haven't kept in touch. John Calvin's and Jonathan Edwards's congregations certainly feared God. Maybe too much so. But is it possible that without some real, honest fear of God, the power of God's redemption in Christ has little meaning? Could it be that this is the reason the women and disciples responded with such joy when Jesus said to them, "Do not be afraid." Gods are to be feared. That's the nature of most religions. The remarkable thing about our God is not that he asked Abraham to sacrifice his son (human sacrifices were common) but that he didn't want Isaac—that he himself provided a lamb. The remarkable thing about our God is that instead of punishing us he sent "his only begotten Son" as a ransom. Until we begin to understand the fear that the Jews felt and the power of sacrifice, this passage will only be preached and heard on a surface level.

Gospel: Luke 24:13–35. In some ways it is difficult for us to get into this story. Difficult for us to understand the disciples' dismay, their anger, their confusion. The story is so familiar, as homey as any good bedtime story. We know this Jesus who came and went and rose. We read the last chapter before we started. We know the outcome. So it's difficult for us to appreciate the disciples' dismay.

But like Cleopas and his friend, we are partially blind. We don't "recognize" him yet, because we are looking for something else—a Jesus we can manipulate, one we can cling to. We look for a charismatic Jesus who will answer our every whim; an intellectual Jesus who will snicker smugly with us at pious faith-talk; a sweet Jesus with no moral sting to his words; a social-action Jesus with no pastoral concern; or a quiet Jesus who gets tucked in our Bibles hiding behind red letters. We want a hero or a superstar. Somewhere along the road he overtakes us, but we don't recognize him because we are looking for someone else. The last thing Cleopas and his friend wanted was a dead Jesus. The cross spelled failure, and nobody likes defeat. No wonder an ecclesiastical journal received so much protest about its front cover one month. It showed a gnarled, unattractive Jesus twisted in pain as he conquers our twisted sin. Christ shatters our expectations of him.

Cleopas and his friend are on their way to Emmaus. "Emmaus may be going to church on Sunday," writes Frederick Buechner in *The Magnificent Defeat* ([New York: Seabury Press, 1966], p. 85). "Emmaus is whatever we do or wherever we go to make ourselves forget that the world holds nothing sacred: that even the wisest and the bravest and loveliest decay and die. . . . Emmaus is where we go, where these two went, to try to forget about Jesus and the great failure of his life." So someone dies and Cleopas and his friend are in church on Sunday to hear the preacher's words. But the preacher speaks of the Christ's death. The words are harsh when the two need pastoral care. "You fools. The Messiah has to die before entering glory. Our risen Lord must first be our suffering Lord. The law and the prophets point to it. But rejoice, for our God has turned a cross of death into a victory sign!" Somehow recognition comes not with the words but with the sign, not with the sermon but with the sacrament. Why did it seem as though he were the host and we the guests in our own home? Perhaps it was the way he took the bread, the way he blessed it and broke it. Whatever the reason, we suddenly understand that when he has gone from the table he no longer wants us to cling to old memories of him (false memories) but to go, proclaim, tell the news. The only way to keep him is to go with him. We go, not merely as individuals but as the church celebrating the risen Lord in word and sacrament.

The Fourth Sunday of Easter

Lutheran	Roman Catholic	Episcopal	Pres/UCC/Chr	Meth/COCU
Acts 6:1–9; 7:2a, 51–60	Acts 2:14, 36–41	Acts 6:1–9; 7:2a, 51–60 or Neh. 9:6–15	Acts 2:36–41	Acts 6:1–9; 7:2a, 51–60 or Neh. 9:6–15
1 Pet. 2:19–25	1 Pet. 2:20b–25	1 Pet. 2:19–25 or Acts 6:1–9; 7:2a, 51–60	1 Pet. 2:19–25	1 Pet. 2:19–25
John 10:1–10	John 10:1–10	John 10:1–10	John 10:1–10	John 10:1–10

EXEGESIS

First Lesson: Acts 6:1–9; 7:2a, 51–60. Here we begin with a passage which brings several traditional titles to consideration, as the account of the institution of the order of deacons, for example, or as the *dies natalis* of the protomartyr of the church. For the author of Acts, it is fairly safe to say that neither of these titles is paramount. It is rather for him an occasion to show how the church began to break out of its strictly Jewish origins in an outreach that would eventually constitute it fully catholic. Stephen foreshadows Paul and the gentile church. So also does the discourse attributed to Stephen, the fifth of Acts, foreshadow in its repudiation of all that was narrowly Jewish the ecumenical preaching of the apostle to the nations.

In v. 1 Luke continues to indicate the growth and diversification of the infant church. The "Hellenists" are Greek-speaking Jews as opposed to the "Hebrews." There is nothing extraordinary about the presence in Jerusalem of these Hellenists, by origin or by descent Jews of the Diaspora from outside Palestine; we know that there was at least one Greek-speaking synagogue in Jerusalem. For the first time, however, we discover that Jewish cultural divisions had been carried over into the church by the converts to Christianity. For Luke this fact presaged the eventual ecumenism of the church. Hence the catalog of names in v. 5, all of which are Greek (unlike the Hebrew or Aramaic names of all the original disciples), and hence in that same verse the notation that one of these was a proselyte from Antioch, that is, he was not a Jew by descent but only by conversion to the religion of Judaism. All this is of greater significance to Acts than determining how the office conferred by the laying on of apostolic hands in v. 6 is related to the later ecclesiastical structures. That office, in view of the distinction made in vv. 2–3, we might think entirely engaged with temporalities, yet such a conclusion is not borne out by subsequent events, when at least two of these designated ministers are soon seen carrying out the selfsame spiritual works of the Twelve.

The same situation that led to Stephen's appointment also leads to his death. The Freedmen were probably descendants of those Jews who had been transported to Rome by Pompey in 63 B.C. and sold into slavery. Later freed, some had returned to Palestine, but they had learned new ways and lived apart from the Hebrews. They doubtless felt more at home among the Diaspora Jews from Cyrene, Alexandria, Cilicia, and Asia. Thus it is that the Hellenistic Jews among whom Stephen the Hellenist is ministering form the opposition to him and eventually slay him, even as the earlier disciples were opposed by their fellow Hebrews.

Of Stephen's discourse at his trial, the longest of the discourses in Acts, we have in this reading only the conclusion. The discourse, in which Christ is never named and appears only by allusion, is not specifically Hellenistic but very Jewish, much in the manner of the OT historical recitals of which we have a good example in Psalm 106. The conclusion in vv. 51–53, in which Stephen accuses his auditors of imitating their fathers in a history of persecution of the prophets, is also not specifically Hellenistic. Significant is v. 56 in which Stephen identifies the glorified Christ of his vision with the Son of man. This is the only instance in the NT (aside, perhaps, from Rev. 1:13) in which this title, habitual on Jesus' lips in the Gospels, is used about him by someone else. It will be remembered that it was under this title that Jesus provoked final condemnation upon himself, according to Luke 22:69. The parallels which Luke habitually draws between Jesus and his apostolic ministers have been particularly sustained in this story of Stephen, beginning with the wonders and signs he worked (6:8), continued in the circumstances of his trial, down to the details of false witnesses suborned to charge him with blasphemy against the temple (6:11–14), and concluding with Stephen's calling on the Lord to receive his spirit and uttering a loud cry (cf. Luke 23:46) while forgiving his afflicters (Luke 23:34).

Second Lesson: 1 Pet. 2:19–25. This passage is a paraenetical address to slaves—who undoubtedly accounted for a great number of the members of the early Christian churches—regarding their duty to be submissive and acquiescent in their state of life. By beginning the reading at v. 19 and omitting v. 18 the lectionary obviously wishes the apostolic admonitions that follow to be taken as applicable to all Christians. The relevance of the christological section enclosed in vv. 22–24 is thereby highlighted all the more.

Unjust suffering, intolerable when permitted by those whose task it is to order society, is nevertheless to be commended to the Christian as a personal choice. The reason for this is not the character-building motivation of Stoicism but rather one that flies in the face of the dictates of natural propriety and equity, namely the example given by Christ. Here is brought in a brief christological reflection which may have been a hymn or other liturgical peroration and almost certainly is a citation by the author. In v. 24 and in the author's conclusion in v. 25 there is a sustained allusion to Isa. 53:5–12. Here, it may be noted, is ascribed a positive value to the suffering of Christ. The doctrine of the cross is clearly asserted—the atoning power of the passion which has made possible a new life unto God in which is true freedom. The Christian is not called precisely to the imitation of Christ, for in truth the Christ event is once for all, and inimitable, but Christ may be taken as a model of forbearance and trust in God in the face of injustice and human malice.

Gospel: John 10:1–10. Today's reading presents a discourse by Jesus, whom on this occasion the Fourth Gospel situates in Jerusalem, presumably at the time of the Feast of Tabernacles (so 7:2, 37, without any subsequent change of season indicated). In 10:22 the Feast of the Dedication is mentioned, a more appropriate setting, one might think, in view of the fact that Ezekiel 34, a description of the divine shepherd, seems to have formed part of the liturgical readings in the Jewish observance of this festival in Jesus' time. In any case, however, the discourse has a timeless quality to it, as do most of the dominical sayings in John's Gospel. There can be no doubt that the Christ who speaks, though he is represented in the circumstances of his earthly ministry, is unmistakably the exalted Lord of the church. There is a mingling of metaphors here that is typically Johannine. Jesus is first of all the one and only door or gate to the sheepfold. One is invited to recall the Palestinian scene where the individual shepherds' flocks were sheltered at night in a communal walled enclosure. The fold was supervised, of course, and no one who was not recognized by the keeper of the gate would be admitted to the sheep;

anyone else, who would obviously be a thief, would have to break in surreptitiously by another way. As the gate, therefore, Jesus is the only legitimate means of access to the sheep, who signify here, as they do so often elsewhere, those called to be God's people. On the one hand, therefore, Jesus is the criterion by which the true shepherds of God's people are to be recognized.

By a shifting of the figure, however, Jesus himself is identified with the true shepherd (cf. Jer. 23:1–9), the one whom the eye of faith will recognize as truly appointed of God. As v. 8 makes clear, he is being contrasted with others who have pretended to reveal God or God's plan ("all who came before me") and is declared to be the only one who has truly been able to give life as one sent by God. Again the figure bespeaks the Palestinian scene, where the shepherd enters the fold to call his sheep by name, who then recognize him and follow him forth into pasture. "All that the Father gives me will come to me; and him who comes to me I will not cast out" (John 6:37).

HOMILETICAL INTERPRETATION

Traditionally, last Sunday was Good Shepherd Sunday. Probably to make room for the Emmaus road story, it has been moved back a week. A hasty glance at the Second Lesson and the Gospel would send the preacher into the pulpit with a topical sermon on the Good Shepherd and his sheep. But unless your congregation works in the high country of New Zealand it could mean very little. And yet—there is more beneath the surface. Examine the passages carefully.

First Lesson: Acts 6:1–9; 7:2a, 51–60. Our readings from Acts this Eastertide have surveyed the church's mission to convert the Jews and the Gentiles. This passage points to those Hellenized Jews who form a bridge between the Jerusalem church and the gentile world. It also goes beyond the question of mission to the problem of administration. Sooner or later jealousies have a way of arising in any parish. Here the widows of the Hellenists weren't getting a fair shake. And as it happens today, those griping were put in charge of dealing with the problem. They were appointed servers—not a bad image for pastors today. It is hard to imagine waiting on tables after all that seminary training. But is that not what we do in Holy Communion? We serve on behalf of the one who served us supremely. It is part of *our* shepherding function.

But in our passage the servers are also preachers. Stephen is the prime example. His sermon (probably not given at one time) turns from history to theology to invective. But notice the omission of a christological emphasis. Stephen rehearses Israel's history and then makes his point about the temple in a quotation from one of the Hebrew prophets (Isa. 66:1-2). The emphasis in Luke is not John's "worship of God in spirit and in truth" or Paul's "living body of Christ." Luke sets up a contrast between a holy-place and a holy-people theology. This Christ, this risen Lord, cannot be confined. Our God cannot be contained in a man-made house. He is out and about. He lives in our hearts, in the church on the move. Those who believed that God resided in only synagogue or church stoned poor Stephen for taking them to task. In Luke's marvelous dramatic style Stephen's garments are laid at the feet of Saul, who himself would later be hounded and driven from town to town by those who rejected the gospel.

Second Lesson: 1 Pet. 2:19-25. If the Acts passage examines a Hebrew-Hellenist conflict, this one uncovers the open sores of labor-management negotiations. Imagine a union boss in Pittsburgh addressing his members this way—especially with v. 18. "Be submissive to your employers. Suffer patiently." An election for a new union boss would be held immediately. But the audience of this letter were neither steelworkers nor machinists. They were workers, yes, but Christians. Even yet it is odd to tell someone that suffering is a Christian virtue, unless one is bucking for a masochism award. Look again. To suffer *unjustly* is the Christian virtue. Here exhortation leads to theology. Again the Christology is more about crucifixion than resurrection. Christ suffered unjustly. The shepherd became a lamb himself and laid down his life for us. He did so without threatening or hating. Here the three passages come together. Stephen followed Christ's example and we Christians are to do the same. One wonders how liberation theologians would read this passage. We can see how oppressed people have the right to revolt. But that is not Christ's example. He rejects all violence. He avoids both active and passive resistance. This text must create real tension for Christian revolutionists. As Bo Reicke suggests, it presents us with an unbridled optimism in the results of nonresistance, in the power of God to liberate his people.

Gospel: John 10:1-10. In the background I hear echoes of "The Lord is my shepherd, I shall not want . . ." Words muttered by clergy at a graveside. Then we begin to understand in the midst of death about having life, abundantly. Those oppressed and persecuted in the

Johannine community could hear these words as full of grace and truth. The risen Christ is the good shepherd. Not only that, he is the gate.

One striking feature in this passage is the mention of voices. The sheep hear the shepherd's voice. They follow him because they *know* his voice. They do not follow strangers because they do not know their voices. Not only that, the shepherd calls them by name. Where else in John's Gospel does this happen? Mary recognizes the risen Christ when he calls her by name. As Walter Brueggemann has suggested, our God does not yell "Hey you!" at us in a crowd. He calls us by name. We hear the voice of God throughout the Bible. Yahweh thunders. There is nothing of the Rogerian, nondirective counselor, about our God. That is, until he stands strangely mute before Pilate. The voice of God in the OT, to be hearkened to and obeyed, becomes in John the voice of a man. God said more than "Let there be light." He said "Let there be a voice." And "the *Word* became flesh and dwelt among us, full of grace and truth." Can you hear the voice of the shepherd? It comes in recognition and in continued care. It may suggest a high doctrine of preaching and pastoral care as God takes our poor, human pulpit words and spells them with a capital *W*.

The Fifth Sunday of Easter

Lutheran	Roman Catholic	Episcopal	Pres/UCC/Chr	Meth/COCU
Acts 17:1–15	Acts 6:1–7	Acts 17:1–15 or Deut. 6:20–25	Acts 6:1–7	Acts 17:1–15 or Deut. 6:20–25
1 Pet. 2:4–10	1 Pet. 2:4–9	1 Pet. 2:1–10 or Acts 17:1–15	1 Pet. 2:4–10	1 Pet. 2:1–10
John 14:1–12	John 14:1–12	John 14:1–14	John 14:1–12	John 14:1–14

EXEGESIS

First Lesson: Acts 17:1–15. This passage is not an apostolic discourse but the narration of a portion of what is conventionally called Paul's second missionary journey. After describing Paul's experiences at Philippi, Luke now details the journey of Paul and Silas down the ancient Egnatian Way through Amphipolis and Apollonia to Thessalonica, where apparently they lodged at the house of a Jew named Jason, building up there the beginning of a Christian church drawn from the local synagogue, including both Jews and proselytes. Thessalonica, then as now, was the second city of Greece, under Roman rule a self-governing democracy in the Greek fashion presided over by representatives whom Luke correctly designates *politarchai* ("city authorities"). Luke seemingly does not approve of this Thessalonian order: though Paul had originally achieved some success in his proclamation of Jesus in the synagogue, it was all too easy for the unbelieving Jews to stir up trouble by inciting the rabble (*agoraioi*, literally, "frequenters of the marketplace") against him, seeking a judgment through lynch law. The charge was a typically demagogic one phrased almost in the same words as that brought against Jesus in his trial before Pilate (cf. Luke 23:2): sedition and treason against Caesar. It is nothing new for Paul to be forced to leave a place he has chosen for his mission: violence in this instance is averted only by his loyal converts who spirit him away. It seems apparent that by Luke's repeated insistence on this theme as well as by the pointed parallel drawn between the apostles' experience and that of Jesus (including the reference to the necessity of Christ's suffering and resurrection in v. 3), Luke is continuing here his missionary theology.

Another Lucan emphasis that can hardly go unnoticed is the note that both at Thessalonica and at Beroea highborn women are prominent among the converts of Paul and Silas. Luke especially among the NT writers is insistent upon the role played by women in the ministry both of Jesus and of the apostolic church. Beroea, the modern Véroia, an old Macedonian country town of settled ways, is obviously more to Luke's taste than the metropolis of Thessalonica. Here the Jews eagerly hear the apostolic word, the unlocking of the meaning of prophecy in the light of the gospel. "To see if these things were so" hardly expresses doubt on the part of the Beroeans but rather amazement and joy. When the inevitable dissension arises that forces Paul's departure, it is not prompted by Beroean dissatisfaction but by troublemakers come down from Thessalonica.

Second Lesson: 1 Pet. 2:1–10. This paraenetical section of 1 Peter continues in some fashion the verses that precede it; however, though it is somewhat loosely organized and moves rather quickly from thought to thought, it forms a satisfying whole of its own.

The exhortation in v. 1 to put away all vices—obviously the list of five is only exemplary—is evidently motivated by the spiritual rebirth spoken of above in 1:23, as the following verses make clear. By their reception of the gospel word, these Christians have become as newborn children, whose sustenance is by their continued acceptance of this word in faith, which will enable them to grow into the adulthood of final salvation. As yet they have but had a first taste, an earnest, of the goodness of the Lord. V. 3 literally: "If you once tasted that the Lord is sweet"—*chrēstos ho kyrios.* Possibly there is a wordplay involved with the Christian acclamation *christos ho kyrios:* "Christ is the Lord."

Certainly Christ is the Lord to whom the author refers, as the following verses make quite clear. The association of ideas and figures in these verses is clear enough, but it is difficult to say which one has led to the other in this almost stream-of-consciousness sequence. Probably it is the christological use made of the various OT "stone" passages, coupled with the notion of faith to which the author has just exhorted, that has determined the development of his thought. Christ is identified with the cornerstone of the new Zion in Isa. 28:16; with the stone rejected by the builders in Ps. 118:22; and with the stone of stumbling of Isa. 8:14. The common denominator of these passages is that the stone represents that which can be either accepted as a sure foundation of security or rejected with the consequence of frustration. For those who accept Christ in faith he is a living stone: living, first and foremost, by his resurrection from the dead, but also life-giving as Lord of the church. Hence those who accept him also become living stones—and here the metaphor moves into the image of a stone house. Implied is a contrast with the temple of Jerusalem, a perishable house made by human hands (cf. Acts 17:24). The spiritual house made up of these living stones, on the contrary, is one which by the power of God grows up into everlasting life. In keeping with its character, and again in contrast with the Jerusalem temple, there are in this house of God no animal sacrifices but only the spiritual sacrifices of the Christian life, in which all the "living stones" make up the only priesthood.

In the final verses the author lets go the stone metaphor and resumes the priestly one enunciated in v. 5. Actually, what dominates these verses is the concept of "a people," which the recipients of this Epistle once were not but now have been constituted through God's grace. A people, in biblical thought, meant not just a gathering or association of individuals but a unity forged out of common interests, language, destiny, and concerns. Paraphrasing Exod. 19:6, God's words to Israel celebrating its constitution as a people in the event of the Exodus from Egypt, the author now spells out for Christians what are the consequences of their election to God's kingdom. For kingdom it is; "kingdom of priests" is the original expression underlying the "royal priesthood" of the Greek translation followed by 1 Peter. Salvation is not a purely personal arrangement of a one-to-one relationship to God. It is a social arrangement in which relationship to

God is achieved through one's membership in a chosen people. The priestly character of this people is twofold, consisting both in the ministry of Christians one to another and in the collective witness of praise and worship of the one who has called them out of the darkness of sin and error into the light of his truth.

Gospel: John 14:1–14. This is the earliest part of the Farewell Discourse (or Testament of Jesus) which in the Fourth Gospel forms the major emphasis of the portrayal of the Last Supper. There are at least three major points of emphasis on which we should dwell.

First, this is a farewell discourse, in which Jesus says that he is departing from the disciples. True, he says in v. 3 that he will return—but only to collect the disciples, so to speak, and take them with him to the place he is now going to prepare for them, namely the dwelling places in his Father's house. This sounds very much like the language of early Christian eschatological hope, according to which the Parousia would usher in a new heaven and earth and the rapture of the righteous into the heavenly Kingdom. But how does such an interpretation square with the remainder of the discourse, with the promise of the coming of the Paraclete who will abide with the disciples forever as Christ's alter ego (v. 16), and with the assurance that Christian love will guarantee not an ascent of Christians to heaven but rather a descent of the Father and the Son to make their dwelling with them (v. 23)? It seems that in these verses John has indeed made use of early eschatological language, but only to adapt it to his more habitual way of viewing the reality of the Christ event. The Christ who speaks in 14:1–14 is the glorified Christ who has already accomplished the task allotted him in God's economy (cf. 13:31). Time dissolves, therefore, in this perspective, even though the old temporal terms are still preserved. The Father's house is already prepared and ready for occupancy and is indistinguishable from the indwelling of Father, Son, and Spirit in the church. This understanding seems to be justified in view of the second point of emphasis that follows.

Belief in Christ in v. 1 is equated with belief in God. Whoever knows Christ, according to v. 7, knows the Father; and according to v. 9, whoever has seen Christ has seen the Father. On the basis of these combinations, one can only reverse the conventional axiom and say that in Johannine terms "believing is seeing." Christ is in the Father and the Father in Christ (vv. 10–11); as we know, John can even have Jesus say that he and the Father are one (10:11). These are not metaphysical statements but rather soteriological ones. They affirm that in the exaltation of Christ, who now lives in the church through the abiding presence of the Spirit, the Kingdom of God has been realized for all who believe. So then the affirmation that Christ is the way, the truth, and the life. "The way," as is known from Qumran and the Acts of the Apostles, was conventional eschatological language for an apocalyptic group with pretensions of standing on the threshold of the end time and of possessing the means of conducting the seeker after righteousness into the ultimate truth and eternal life. It is in this sense that "way" appears in v. 4, in a display of Johannine irony. But after Thomas's predictably puzzled interrogation in v. 5, the disciple assuming precisely the role of the seeker after righteousness, in v. 6 Jesus triumphantly asserts that he himself is the way—and therefore he himself is the truth and the life also of eschatological expectation.

Finally, what are we to make of the assertion, in v. 12, that the disciples of Jesus, those who believe in him, will not only do his works but will do greater works than his? What work can be greater than the work of Christ by which the whole world has been redeemed? None, of course, unless it be understood to be at the same time Christ's work, a continuation of the work of Christ-in-the-church ("because I go to the Father"). The work of the historical Jesus, a perspective to which John clings in his Gospel even though his Christ speaks in the language of early Christianity, was restricted to a tiny backwater of the then all-encompassing Roman Empire. The work of early Christianity was already being felt throughout the length and breadth of that empire and was affecting peoples undreamed of in the Palestine of Jesus' time. We cannot avoid the impression that for the Fourth Evangelist more and greater are the same: the works of the disciples are greater than those of their Master because, even though they remain his works, through him they have achieved a scope which historical circumstances had denied him. This little section is often invoked to testify to "the power of Christian prayer." It does this, provided we understand what is involved in "asking the Father in the name of Jesus." In John's Gospel "name" has its full Semitic sense, to represent the person itself (cf. 17:6): to pray in Jesus' name is to act in consort and in communion with him.

HOMILETICAL INTERPRETATION

As we move through this season the empty tomb seems to get further and further away. The meaning of the resurrection and the risen Lord seems to be a matter for the church and our Christian lives more than a matter of a ghostly Savior appearing here and there. That is certainly true today. The concern in our passages is not with a rolled-back stone but with the cornerstone and living stones; not with the way out of the tomb but with the way to the Father.

It would be easy to preach several sermons this Sunday. The difficulty will be choosing which one. No central theme emerges. There is the significance of belief in Jesus in the Second Lesson and Gospel. But each passage addresses the problem from different angles, just as they do do in the matter of housing—the spiritual house and "my Father's house."

First Lesson: Acts 17:1–15. Paul and his entourage are making their way across Macedonia setting their little gospel fires everywhere they go. Paul seems to live for controversy. Actually he lives for the gospel, and that creates controversy. He preached "Christ crucified and risen" to people who found the cross a scandal. Not only that, he was a supply preacher three Sundays (Sabbaths) in a row. He is the center of our drama. Paul, the persecuter of Christians, now preaches the Christian message. Paul the persecuter for the Jewish authorities, now puts them on the defensive. How quickly the scene has changed from last week's reading. Stephen's clothes were dumped at Saul's feet. Now Saul with a new name and a new vocation is preaching the very message that brought Stephen down with stones. Why? He has seen the light. The risen Lord transforms lives. Don't get sidetracked and preach on "Paul's appeal to the upper classes and women." Both are significant but not central here.

Paul shows, as the lessons have throughout this season, that the prophets promised this Messiah. And this Messiah is the Jesus who was crucified and whom God raised. Here is the message that angered the descendants of Abraham and Isaac. Following Paul from town to town, they represent not the Jew today, but anyone trying to stamp out the spreading word of the risen Lord. Just as Herod failed in his attempt to smother the coming of the Lord, all soon discover that the flames of the Christian movement cannot be extinguished, especially when fanned by the Spirit of Christ. The breath of God keeps the church alive, even in the midst of persecution.

Second Lesson: 1 Pet. 2:1–10. Cornelius has been here. Thomas and the two on the road have been here. Could it be that this Sunday those recently baptized, those who joined the church during Holy Week, are here trying to find out what they are supposed to do now? The first thing they hear coming to church is imperatives. "Put away" all malice, guile, insincerity, envy, and slander—all those inclinations toward evil. The moral responsibility of their new life in Christ is addressed at the outset. How do they do it? By drinking the pure milk of Christ's word, by accepting their infancy in the faith. Here milk means continual nourishment, not rudimentary doctrine as in 1 Cor. 3:2.

Suddenly the image shifts from child care to buildings and construction work. The contracts with Israel are renewed. The temple Stephen preached against in Acts 7, quoting Isa. 66:1–2 as his authority, is now replaced by a spiritual house with us as living stones and Christ as the living cornerstone. "Spiritual sacrifices" (v. 5) replace the sacrifices of animals, a theme taken from Hebrew prophecy (see for example Ps. 51:16–17; Mic. 6:6–8). That is the nature of our priesthood. We often think of the church as the building. Consider how much time and money is spent with the building committee. But what of the spiritual life committee, if indeed there is such a thing? Parishes have ceremonies laying cornerstones when they build a new sanctuary. But do they remember the true cornerstone? Is Jesus the cornerstone a stumbling block for us as much as for Jews? If we are guilty of commission here, we are guilty of omission in the area of sacrifice. The emphasis is clearly on living the gospel daily.

What shall we do with all those titles in v. 9? Simple. We "declare the wonderful deeds of him who called" us out of darkness into that marvelous light. We proclaim our adoption. No longer are we orphans or strangers. We are God's own people. If you look carefully just behind this passage and these metaphors, you can see the early church struggling with ways to describe its experience and mission. Isn't it interesting that the newly baptized and some of us veterans are still struggling?

Gospel: John 14:1–14. John is the master of mixed metaphors. If in other places he chooses word, light, bread, vine, here he selects way, truth, and life. He puts them in a shaker and dumps them out. But somehow all his theological scrabble words make sense in Jesus. The various levels and layers of meaning are only clear to the eyes of faith. As Professor Vawter points out, you have to believe it to see it. Keep a close eye on Jesus and you will begin to understand. If Paul had the main role in the Acts passage, Jesus is center stage here. Actually, we never would have heard of Paul if Jesus had not first played the leading role in the drama of salvation history. Here we meet Jesus coming and going. In fact, all his comings and goings come together in this passage. We get only a glimpse of this young man's ministry; not the earthly Jesus but the glorified Christ in John. There is no question that the spotlight is on him. Even he seems to know it in John's Gospel. We cannot miss the "I am" sayings here unique to John. The frequency of the Greek *egō* here does not mean that Jesus is egocentric and lacks humility, but that the theology of the Johannine community is Christocentric. If our Christian lives and our ecclesiology were Christocentric, perhaps we would not lack humility. Perhaps we could see and know the Father.

Jesus and John obviously think it is important to "know the Father." They presume that here. Of course it is important. Like prodigals we have been estranged, have become separated from God our Father. Jesus is the way back to him. He does not point the way. The Baptist, down by the riverside, did that. He *is* the way. He is the way because he is truth and life. "Way" has to do with our relationship with the Father. "Truth" and "life" tell us something about Jesus. It's all laid out—seems simple enough; almost a three-point sermon.

But somehow we still don't understand. Why does he have to go? With Thomas and Philip, our questions go on. Without Jesus around what will *we* be able to do? The fact is, he is around in his Spirit; and with him we do greater works than he did in his earthly life. Somehow that's hard to believe, but true. So believe, and then act in his name. We act and ask in his name. Because of Christ, God can never be a stranger again—the stranger in the shadows whose face we cannot see and whose voice is barely audible. Because of Christ, we know our Father and by his Spirit do his works.

The Sixth Sunday of Easter

Lutheran	Roman Catholic	Episcopal	Pres/UCC/Chr	Meth/COCU
Acts 17:22–31	Acts 8:5–8, 14–17	Acts 17:22–31 or Isa. 41:17–20	Acts 8:4–8, 14–17	Acts 17:22–31 or Acts 8:4–8, 14–17 or Isa. 41:17–20
1 Pet. 3:15–22	1 Pet. 3:15–18	1 Pet. 3:8–18 or Acts 17:22–31	1 Pet. 3:13–18	1 Pet. 3:8–22
John 14:15–21	John 14:15–21	John 15:1–8	John 14:15–21	John 14:15–21

EXEGESIS

First Lesson: Acts 17:22–31. The question whether Paul ever actually addressed the Areopagus in Athens is idle and frivolous if statistical rather than theological fact is considered to be the paramount issue for the author of Acts. What is of the utmost importance is that in this passage possibly the most ecumenical of all the NT authors has represented the apostle to the Gentiles preaching the gospel not merely *to* them but also *of* them, that is, asking them not to hear an alien history of salvation drawn from a religious experience not their own, but to hearken to the traditions of their own people to see how compatible they were with the good news recently revealed in far-off Judea. There is here no compromise of the gospel, only an empathy with the historical Paul, as his own letters have revealed him, insisting that one need not first be made a Jew in order then to become a Christian. The historical Paul insisted that for gentile Christians the ritual and law of Judaism could be dispensed with, but he himself lived by its history and tradition, its Scripture, which seems to have been his only literature. The author of Acts, if we read him correctly, feels that this history and tradition also could be dispensed with in subordination to the priority of the gospel. Paul, the inspired pragmatist (cf. Phil. 1:18), would probably not have disagreed; but Luke has certainly gone beyond anything that Paul personally wrote on the subject.

In Athens Paul was at last (after Macedonia) in the real Greece, in the school city of Greco-Roman culture. As is usually the case, Luke's mise-en-scène is meticulously authentic. Paul's argument in the agora, after his initial contact with Jews and proselytes, with "the Epicurean and Stoic philosophers" (v. 18), is indeed a picture taken out of contemporary life. These were the ordinary Athenians with whom one might be thought to come into contact in the city: "philosophers," then as now, must be accorded the title simply on their own recognizance. Epicureanism was, so to speak, the religion of the practical man, not a hedonism as it has frequently been caricatured but rather a way of life premised on enlightened self-interest. Stoicism was an equally materialistic system of thought which, however, added to the individualism of Epicureanism the notions of service and the brotherhood of man, ideas which it derived from a fuzzy superimposed pantheism. (There is a temptation to translate these rather vague ideologies of first-century Greece into the equally misleading contemporary terminology of "conservative" and "liberal.") At any rate, Paul is regarded by these people as a "babbler," literally a "magpie," and more literally yet a "picker of seeds" *(spermalogos)*, a word borrowed from Athenian slang signifying an itinerant speaker. This, be it noted, not to his discredit: for as Luke correctly observes and as late observers have corroborated ever since, "the Athenians and the foreigners who live there spend their time in nothing except telling or hearing something new." The "something new" which Paul was preaching was "Jesus and the resurrection" which, according to v. 18, were taken to be "foreign deities": *Iesous kai he Anastasis* might so have been construed by a pagan mind attuned to divine consorts male and female. Paul's discourse is a model of diplomacy and accommodation.

First, the Athenians are "very religious"—superstitious, of course, to the extent that they must offer sacrifice to an unknown god, lest any jealous deity might have been overlooked in their orisons. (An actual inscription of the Palatine hill in Rome proclaimed an altar *sive deo sive deae sacrum,* "consecrated to either god or goddess," possibly indicating a more practical Roman attitude fearful of female as well as of male divine retribution.) Paul takes the attitude in good part, however. The Athenians wanted to worship God, only who he really is was unknown to them. Who is this God?

He is (1) *the one "who made the world and everything in it"*—a contradiction of the easy or semireflective materialism of both Epicureanism and Stoicism. (2) *He dwells not in "shrines made by man."* If Paul actually delivered this sermon on the *areios pagos,* the Hill of Mars overlooking the agora of Athens where at present a stone text in NT and modern Greek commemorates the occasion, down in the valley were exposed numerous august marble shrines, beautiful in architecture but as monuments of superstition contradictory to the enlightened philosophy of his auditors. (3) True, the contemporary Epicureans would hold that the divine principle they acknowledged needs nothing; but in contradiction to their belief, *God gives to all men life and breath and everything"—he is not indifferent to the world,* and he contradicts their deism. (4) With the Stoics it must be agreed that all men are one. But with what practical consequence, if any? Paul can see none unless the Greeks are willing to listen to their own scriptures: there follow quotations from pagan writings (Epimenides of Knossos, sixth century B.C., for one; the Stoic Aratus of Cilicia, third century B.C., for another) which testified to the conclusions of respected thinkers that nature itself proclaimed *a personal Creator God.* (It must be remembered that Homer and Hesiod were considered in Greek society to have the same character that the Jews ascribed to their own sacred books. Paul—or Luke—is here simply extending this pagan canon.) These premises being accepted, how foolish is idolatry or the notion that divinity can be captured in material terms.

Up to this point, probably nothing has been said that would not correspond with the Athenians' cultural experience, just as Stephen's speech, for example, said nothing that did not correspond in every detail to the cultural experience of Israel. Now, however, comes the gospel—to which all the foregoing has been propaedeutic—the good news for which there has been no preparation except a hoped-for receptivity to divine revelation. In this case (cf. vv. 32–34) the gospel is greeted with the same mingled bemusement, rejection, and belief that it had achieved among the Jews.

The gospel that Paul preaches: the times of ignorance are past, and there must be repentance for sin against the coming judgment of the world through one who has been appointed and certified judge by his resurrection from the dead.

Second Lesson: 1 Pet. 3:8–22. The Petrine lesson for the preceding Sunday began with a paraenetical section referring to five vices to be avoided. This one begins with five homely virtues which are commended, along with a citation (in vv. 10–12) of Ps. 34:12–16 (according to the Septuagint translation). The message is a simple one, which is saved from sententiousness, however, by the consideration that the admonition to return good for evil (v. 9) is addressed to the real situation of people actually undergoing persecution and slander.

The vade mecum that follows, "how to act in time of persecution," is a mingling of traditional wisdom and christological consciousness. The author holds to the prevalent OT view that in principle it is evildoers who are punished in this life (cf. 2:14). Nevertheless, he recognizes that it is sometimes God's will that the righteous should suffer and in fact that their righteousness should be the very reason for their suffering. In such a situation the only proper response is to persevere in righteousness, not merely that evil men be put to shame for their inability to convert the persecuted to their own ways, but more importantly because such is the only consistent mode of conduct for one who would follow Christ.

A christological passage is brought in, in v. 18, because Christ is for the author the supreme example of the righteous person who suffers unjustly. The author resumes his reflections derived from this example in 4:1. Obviously, however, the passage has a theological content quite independent of its casual exemplary usage here. Though it is not unusual for 1 Peter to move rapidly from subject to subject and to make frequent digressions, it seems in this instance highly probable that the author has incorporated in vv. 18–22 a baptismal liturgy or homily that once had an independent existence of its own. Furthermore, vv. 18 and 22, which begin and end the passage, have a hymnic character that might point to their having once also been a unity in themselves. The christological affirmations, as they now appear in the Epistle, are: (1) there is vicarious atonement for sin through Christ's (suffering and) death; (2) he was put to death in the flesh but given new life in the spiritual realm (cf. Rom. 1:3–4); (3) he is now exalted in heaven over all angelic powers (cf. Phil. 2:9–10). The somewhat puzzling qualification of the effect of Baptism in v. 21 as "an appeal to God for a clear conscience" appears to be an attempt to discount any temptation to ascribe to it a magical force such as was claimed for other purificatory rites of the time. In keeping with OT precedent (for example, the passage through the Sea of Reeds at the time of the Exodus) a typology for salvation "through water" is found in the story of the flood and Noah's ark (which was actually for Noah and his family a salvation *in spite of* water). This typological precedent also illumines the representation of the resurrected Jesus as preaching to the spirits ("in prison") of those who had been unbelieving in Noah's time. Though the verse is the origin of medieval speculation about "the harrowing of hell" or "the limbo of the fathers," the author's purpose in adapting this theme from the Enoch legend appears to be mainly to stress the fewness of those saved at that time as a cautionary example for his readers.

Gospel: John 14:15–21. In the commentary on the Gospel for the preceding week sufficient was said about the spirit and perspective of these verses, which merely continue the discourse there begun.

The only new note that is introduced in v. 15 has regard to keeping the commandments of Christ. Keeping the commandments means to live in love of God and the community (cf. 15:12–13); it is the indispensable condition for the presence of the Spirit in the church and for the indwelling of Father and Son as well. In such a way does Jesus manifest himself: again for John, believing is seeing. In contrast, the unbelieving world can neither receive the Spirit nor see God or Jesus.

HOMILETICAL INTERPRETATION

As we near the end of Eastertide, we are beginning to round the first bend in the church year. The presence of the risen Christ among us, a central theme of this season, is being understood as less and less dependent on his appearances. The appearances are now merely signaling a deeper, more lasting presence. Our Lord's ascension is almost in sight. Maybe now we can bear his leaving.

This Sunday we find Paul in Athens, Jesus in Hades, and the Paraclete in us. What a combination of passages to preach. The connections among them are loose but evident in places.

First Lesson: Acts 17:22–31. Do you see the pattern that is emerging this season? Look at all the accounts of speeches and sermons we have read. In every case someone is preaching the gospel in one form or another. From Peter at Cornelius's house to Peter at Pentecost,

from Stephen before the Jewish High Council to Paul in a synagogue
and now on Mars Hill, we should not forget that like their Lord, all
were finally killed for their words. There is some risk to preaching
what we believe. Is there still?

In today's passage Paul, the orator, is giving a lesson in persuasion.
On occasion in classes of rhetoric this speech is used as a classic
example of convincing a potentially antagonistic audience by appeal-
ing to common interests. Like John Kennedy advising Houston
clergy on why religion should not be a factor in the 1960 presidential
campaign ("there was no religious test at the Alamo"), Paul strides up
on the hill and begins, "Men of Athens, I perceive that in every way
you are very religious. For as I passed along . . ."

Actually this passage is more than an example of persuasive public
speaking or presenting cogent arguments. It is a commentary on
missionary preaching and the different forms that it took. Here Paul
does not begin with the Jewish promise. There are no Jews in the
audience, so he must find a point of contact—the fact that they are
very religious. In every way many in our society are very religious.
Not as openly religious as Cornelius, maybe. But there is a nagging
curiosity, even in this age of the secular city and post-Christendom.
Jacques Ellul argues this convincingly in *The New Demons*. Human
beings are at bottom very religious. Read Hedrick Smith's description
(in his book *The Russians)* of young Communists pouring out of
a dance about midnight on Easter Eve fascinated by the all-night
paschal liturgy reaching a peak at the adjacent twelfth-century Cathe-
dral of the Assumption in Vladimir. Each of us has inside a repressed
desire for ritual, for worship. So there are the Athenians ready to
worship but not sure whom to worship. Here they come Sunday
morning—willfully ignorant of God but worshiping him. Not just a
congregation in a college town—educated, sophisticated. The curious
and inquisitive are in every parish on Sunday morning. They bring
their questioning minds, their troubled souls, and their willful and
rationalizing disobedience—their calculated idolatry. Is this what
agnostic means? In every way they are very religious and very
curious, worshiping God but not yet really knowing him. Like Paul,
we have to make a point of contact. Preevangelism often precedes
evangelism. And then we preach the gospel—the power of the risen
Lord. The way to know God is to see this Jesus who was crucified and
raised. Do not be surprised if again the message is met with blank
stares or glazed eyes, or possibly humor or confusion. Paul faced the
same response. Perhaps the Athenians are not in church at all but
milling about the college commons or rushing about the shopping
malls. Like Schleiermacher's "cultured despisers," they show a

willful lack of interest in really knowing the God they pretend to worship. Wherever they are, it's our responsibility to proclaim the word in their hearing and to believe that only God can effect conversion through the power of the Holy Spirit.

Second Lesson: 1 Pet. 3:8–22. There are some congregations in the United States that omit the phrase "He descended into hell" from the Apostles' Creed. When you go to preach in one of these churches, the kind lay person who meets you at the door and tells you about the liturgy inevitably says at some point, "Now we don't descend into hell in our church." You never quite know what to say.

There are not many sermons preached on hell these days. The idea of hell is foreign and confusing. The idea of our Lord's going down into Hades is even more repulsive. It is bad enough that he had to die. What does he do in the midst of suffering? James Stewart in *The Strong Name* ([Edinburgh: T. & T. Clark, 1940], p. 24) asked it this way: "In those silent hours . . . when heaven and earth seemed hushed and in suspense, where was Jesus? . . . He was still about his Father's business." He was preaching to the spirits in prison. He preaches to us in our persecution, in the netherworld of our sin. He calls us to suffer for righteousness' sake, to have unity. We are even called to preach to the "spirits in prison" in our age as Paul did in Athens. Our Baptism in Christ makes all of this possible. Somehow knowing that Jesus was raised and exalted gives us new courage and helps us live with "He descended into hell."

At a Good Friday service not too long ago, the leader began reciting the Nicene Creed. Not knowing it as well as the Apostles' Creed, the congregation grabbed for their hymnbooks and caught up with the leader only to find that she stopped with the words "He suffered and was buried." The congregation went on for a phrase: "And the third day he rose again." Voices trailed off but the phrase echoed in the little church. No one there wanted to leave it with "He suffered and was buried." Thank God that he didn't leave it there either.

Gospel: John 14:15–21. The fear of being left alone is very real, and not merely in our age. It is one of the marks of the human spirit. A small child playing in a room is comforted by a parent saying honestly, "I'll be right back." But even as adults, when parents die, we feel abandoned. We know deep down that this time they won't be "right back." For a moment we feel orphaned, suddenly on our own. At the cemetery we feel a little cheated, forsaken. Should we be surprised that the Son of God would know of our problem? Not really, especially in John. John's Jesus knows all. The disciples will not be left alone. Christ's "I'll be right back" comes with the giving of the Spirit. The assurance is more theological than psychological. There is something here for John's community as the eyewitnesses begin to die out. Again we find John's theme about sight coming with insight. His point sounds remarkably like the secret that Saint-Exupery's little prince learned from the fox—the secret about essential things being invisible to the eye but not to the heart. The world cannot *see* Jesus any more than the Athenians (in Acts) can *know* God. But the disciples *see* and *know* God because they love him. That is his main commandment.

We have been spending a lot of time this Eastertide examining what Jesus can do for us. In a consumer society this is significant. Now what can we do for him? We can love him. He is as jealous as Yahweh on Sinai. But the commandment to love him is set in the context to love one another. Love of God leads to love for one another. Even the Second Lesson picks up this theme. But notice that here love for one another begins with love within the Christian community. It is not the Matthean "Love your enemies." We have to begin mending the tears in the body of Christ before we can move out into the world. We can't sing "they'll know we are Christians by our love" unless we Christians love each other. Here is the real test of our love for Christ. How do we treat the rest of his children (who were once orphaned but are no longer)?

The Ascension of Our Lord

Lutheran	Roman Catholic	Episcopal	Pres/UCC/Chr	Meth/COCU
Acts 1:1–11	Acts 1:1–11	Acts 1:1–11 or Dan. 7:9–14	Acts 1:1–11	Acts 1:1–11 or Dan. 7:9–14
Eph. 1:16–23	Eph. 1:17–23	Eph. 1:15–23 or Acts 1:1–11	Eph. 1:16–23	Eph. 1:15–23
Luke 24:44–53	Matt. 28:16–20	Luke 24:49–53 or Mark 16:9–15, 19–20	Luke 24:44–53	Matt. 28:16–20 or Luke 24:44–53

EXEGESIS

First Lesson: Dan. 7:9–14. It is generally agreed that the Book of Daniel is the only truly apocalyptic work in the OT, a work written for the consolation of the persecuted Jewish people of Palestine and reflecting the conditions immediately preceding the Maccabean revolt, in the time of the Seleucid King Antiochus Epiphanes IV

(167–163 B.C.). Our passage comes from the second part of the book, a series of four visions narrated in the first person by the traditional folk hero Daniel, after whom the work has been named.

The preliminary to the apocalyptic vision of our passage is the representation in a dream of four great beasts who rise from the sea, symbolizing by a conventional stylization the successive world empires of recent history: Babylonia (a lion with eagle's wings: a "cherub"), Media (a bear), Persia (a leopard), and finally the Hellenistic Empire. The fourth beast, seemingly too terrible to be adequately described, possesses ten horns. Afterward a little horn appears displacing others: it is the successor kings in the Hellenistic dynasties, specifically the Seleucid dynasties of Syria, and even more specifically the usurping Antiochus within these dynasties, who constituted for the Jews such a fearsome thing out of Alexander's original dream of an ecumenical world. These verses give perspective to the vision of judgment and exaltation that follows.

In general terms the rest of the imagery is fairly transparent. The divine Judge ("one that was ancient of days") sits in condemnation of the world empires. The fourth of these is destined to be utterly destroyed, while of the remainder only powerless remnants will survive. To take their place, and in obvious contrast with the feral figures which have preceded him, now appears with the clouds of heaven "one like a son of man," to whom is given universal dominion and an everlasting kingdom. All this is explained, perhaps needlessly, by an angelic interpreter in the second part of the chapter. The author's expectation evidently envisions not merely a divine judgment against Israel's enemies in the teeth of the contemporary experience that seemed to promise Jewish extinction (v. 25), but it looks as well to a worldwide Judaism that will embrace all the nations, in the manner of Isa. 66:18–21.

In view of the purely typological use made of this passage in the lectionary of this day, it seems hardly necessary to pursue in further detail its historical interpretation.

Second Lesson: Eph. 1:15–23. By many modern authors Ephesians is considered to be Pauline only indirectly, at second hand, and indeed many consider "Ephesians" itself to be a secondary title for a letter or treatise that was originally more general in intent. Such questions hardly affect the interpretation of the present passage, which is an important NT statement of the theological consequences of the exaltation of Christ for both the individual Christian and the church.

The passage begins with a thanksgiving, one of the standard parts of an epistolary introduction, in this case a thanksgiving for the recipients' manifest faith. The thanksgiving speedily becomes a prayer for their further progress in this faith. Though it might appear that a greater than usual stress is laid on the intellective side of the religion here—"a spirit of wisdom and of revelation in the knowledge of him"—we quickly recognize that there is nothing at all Gnostic involved. The wisdom and knowledge for which Paul prays are not theoretical but altogether experiential and practical. Earlier (in v. 14) he had called the Holy Spirit's evident presence among these believers the guarantee (*arrabon,* literally "the down payment") of their final inheritance with Christ. It is knowledge—acknowledgment and recognition and deepened experience of this present salvific reality of life in the Spirit—that is the object of Paul's prayer for the Ephesians.

Such a life has been made possible through the resurrection and exaltation of Christ. In addition to the conventional terms in which this exaltation is expressed ("at the right hand" of God, "in heavenly places," over the angelic powers, "above every name"—cf. Phil. 2:9–11), an ecclesial note is stressed: he is head over all things "for the church." Further, the church is qualified, only here and in Colossians, as Christ's body. This figure does more than simply indicate the organic nature of the church. It also suggests that the life in the Spirit is not one of hope and expectation only but is as well an experienced reality through present union with the glorified Christ. This thought is not far removed from the "realized eschatology" of John. In opposition to the church conceived of as the body of Christ is the statement that it is "the fulness of him who fills all in all." "Fulness" *(pleroma)* in this acceptation is God himself, as he can be possessed by and as he possesses others (cf. 3:19; also Col. 1:19; 2:9). By union with Christ its head the church incarnates God.

Gospel: Luke 24:49–53. Of all the NT writers only Luke has represented the exaltation of Christ as a visible ascension into heaven. Whether he actually did so in this present passage is uncertain, since the "and was carried up into heaven" of v. 51 is not too well attested in the NT manuscripts and may be the result of an attempt by scribes to harmonize these verses with the passage from Acts which is the First Lesson for next Sunday. These verses form the transition between the Gospel of Jesus Christ and the Acts (termed the Gospel of the Spirit from patristic times) by showing Jesus' leave-taking of the disciples, who are bidden to await the coming of the Holy Spirit, and by noting that the temple where the gospel began (1:8–23) has now become a place of Christian prayer. In Acts, following the Pentecostal experience, the apostolic mission will begin from the temple (Acts 3:1).

HOMILETICAL INTERPRETATION

Until the second half of the fourth century ascension was celebrated on Easter Day. From then to now it has been commemorated on the fortieth day after Easter. Stretching the story across several Sundays would be wrong, however, if we were only trying to make a historical point. But we aren't, any more than Christmas followed by Epiphany are dates selected to keep an ancient calendar of the events of the historical Jesus. Many in the early church saw resurrection and ascension as one total event. Early Christian art attests to that fact. One ancient Roman Christian carving shows Mary and three other women in front of the large sepulcher with a Roman guard sleeping close by. In the upper right-hand corner the risen Christ is ascending into heaven while two apostles cower in amazement—one standing up, the other burying his head in fear. Christ seems pulled up a mountain by the hand extending from the cloud in the corner. It is clear from this picture that the power of God is at work. In fact, the unifying theme for today's passages is God's power over evil, over the world (including all nature and history), and over the church—not to mention our own poor lives, as insignificant as they may seem set against the magnificence of these visions.

First Lesson: Dan. 7:9–14. One does not just "read" apocalyptic literature. One tumbles into it like Alice into Wonderland. It is difficult not to stumble about staring up in astonishment. In Daniel 7 we have entered something akin to the fantasy world of Tolkien's Middle Earth. We see fiery thrones and flaming wheels and throngs of thousands, yea, ten thousands. One like a son of man comes with clouds of heaven and has dominion over all, and that means all. Don't miss the fairy-tale language. It permeates the passage. But this is no fairy tale. This vision paints a picture of God's power. Dream interpretation is a dangerous business. Even Joseph knew that. Historical details are only peripherally important as long as one avoids stepping on hermeneutical toes by resisting allegorical inclinations. The tricky thing here is being true to the OT but not stopping short with it. Pair this passage with a NT one before you preach it. Not to do so would mean being untrue to both the OT and the Christian gospel.

One point of interest at the end of v. 14 should not be overlooked.

God's Kingdom shall not pass away. Others have, but his will not. What kind of word is that for us who think that the church's survival depends on our great achievements of evangelism and administration? Should we always scurry about frantically worrying about the church being one generation away from extinction? One wonders about our belief and trust in the power of God.

Second Lesson: Eph. 1:15–23. Earlier we talked of the up-and-down movement of this season—Jesus up on the cross, down into the grave, up Easter morning, now up into heaven. More than spatial and temporal designations, these are theological directions used to describe God's activity in Christ. They also describe God's potential activity in us because Christ is our head. This is not merely something interesting to think about. It is something to live by. You can bank on it. If we find it hard to get up in the morning to be about the Lord's business, it may be that we have a limited vision of Christ's "upness"—his ascension and exaltation. This, of course, means more than getting "high" on Jesus. Jesus is more than someone who got high on God, so to speak. Jesus was raised and departed. But he didn't leave us. He filled us with his presence, the way a body receives life from the head. An infant is helpless, with arms and legs and a body almost completely dysfunctional. But the head is alive, taking nourishment for the rest of the body. As the child grows, the other parts gain strength, but the head continues to see and hear to protect the body. So with the church with Christ as its head. Only in the gospel can we move so comfortably from vertical movement to body talk as the author of Ephesians does in this one long sentence.

Gospel: Luke 24:49–53. Here the scene changes from the grand visions of Daniel and Ephesians to this less pretentious Lucan picture. It's quieter and simpler. Our Lord and his disciples together and then apart. There is no on-the-scene report of the takeoff, as if the disciples had gathered at an ancient Cape Canaveral. In fact, the ascension itself is obscured by Christ's being "carried away" appearing only in variant readings. He simply slips away as in Emmaus. He slips away with a blessing again. Maybe the point is that we should not get too *carried away* with the spectacle and miss the fact that God is acting in this event. Whether "carried away" is authentic or not it is clear that the power of God stands out in this passage. God raises Jesus and exalts him. God empowers us. All this missionary preaching we've been talking about this season—all this *didache* for the newly baptized—can only be done with God's help. Don't miss this point.

There's another point here. Jesus says that we are witnesses to these things. I guess that is true. One Protestant worship book calls the funeral service "Witness to the Resurrection." Standing quietly over a tomb should remind us of the empty tomb. James Dickey, in his description in *God's Images* (Birmingham, Ala.: Oxmoor House, 1977) of Marvin Hayes's etching of the ascension, sees the eternal transfiguration of the whole idea of the tomb: "No longer are graves places to which we have been doomed, but locations from which we rise light." If that's not a gospel word, I'm not sure what is. No wonder the disciples "were continually in the temple blessing God."

The Seventh Sunday of Easter

Lutheran	Roman Catholic	Episcopal	Pres/UCC/Chr	Meth/COCU
Acts 1:(1–7) 8–14	Acts 1:12–14	Acts 1:(1–7) 8–14 or Ezek. 39:21–29	Acts 1:12–14	Acts 1:1–14 or Ezek. 39:21–29
I Pet. 4:12–17; 5:6–11	I Pet. 4:13–16	1 Pet. 4:12–19 or Acts 1:(1–7) 8–14	I Pet. 4:12–19	1 Pet. 4:12–19
John 17:1–11	John 17:1–11a	John 17:1–11	John 17:1–11	John 17:1–11

EXEGESIS

First Lesson: Acts 1:1–14. Luke has provided an elaborate and highly artistic introduction to Acts which highlights its continuity with the Gospel in any number of significant ways. (1) The salutation is to that same Theophilus to whom the Gospel was dedicated. (2) Although Luke alone of the NT writers has allowed a forty-day interval between resurrection and ascension (v. 3; contrast John 20:17) and has represented the latter visually (v. 9), the "day when he was taken up" of v. 2 is probably the same as that of Luke 9:51, referring there to the entirety of the prophetic destiny which Jesus was to fulfill in Jerusalem after his "doing and teaching." (3) As in the Gospel (cf. Luke 24:36–43), the reality of the resurrection demonstrated through the appearances is stressed ("while eating with them" is probably a better reading in v. 4 than the "while staying with them" of RSV). (4) "The promise of the Father" (v. 4) is the Holy Spirit. Just as he separates resurrection and glorification, though the two form a salvific whole, so Luke separates, at least at times, the gift of the Spirit from the rest of the Christ mystery, and he represents this gift in varying ways. Here the sequence is established: baptism of John, Jesus of the Gospel; resurrected Jesus, baptism of the Spirit. (5) The disciples inquire about the establishment of God's reign in traditional Jewish terms: "restore the kingdom to Israel." Jesus redefines it in Christian terms; they are, through the power of the Spirit, to be "witnesses in Jerusalem and in all Judea and Samaria and to the end of the earth." (6) The two men in white robes who announce the ascension and the Parousia are doubtless intended to be the same who attested to the resurrection (Luke 24:4). (7) After the disciples' return to Jerusalem—which they have never really left, since they have been only a Sabbath day's journey away—they repair to the upper room, presumably a well-known place, and therefore probably the same as that where they had eaten the Passover with Jesus (Luke 22:12). (8) Finally, there is a presentation of the initial dramatis personae of Acts, the apostolic band essentially as in Luke 6:14–16 minus Judas Iscariot, and "the women and Mary the mother of Jesus," who had followed him from Galilee and seen the empty tomb, and the brothers of Jesus (James will play an important role in Acts).

Second Lesson: 1 Pet. 4:12–19. The author resumes his treatise on the suffering of persecution, a thing which on no account should come as a surprise to the Christian but rather is what is to be expected in a world that brought suffering on the innocent Christ. Suffering is not to be romanticized either negatively or positively. On the one hand it is something very real, a "fiery ordeal," not to be borne out of simple stoic virtue or welcomed for its supposed therapeutic values. It is a bad thing, and the only occasion of joy that it can afford a Christian is in the opportunity to share the life of Christ, in his degradation as well as in his glory. On the other hand, neither does suffering offer any testimony to virtue, for it may be inflicted very justly for any variety of wrongdoing (cf. 2:14). Not suffering, therefore, but only the consciousness of doing God's will is the criterion of one's ability to withstand the divine judgment. This judgment is imminent, for those who profess Christ as for all others. The former are in the way of salvation and the latter are not; there is no doubt about that. They who suffer now as true Christians may justly regard their suffering as a token of election, a source of confidence that should cancel out their present pain.

Gospel: John 17:1–11. This passage begins the final section of Jesus' farewell discourse according to John, a section in which Jesus no longer speaks to his disciples but rather to God his Father. From very early times this section has been called Christ's priestly prayer, and such it is, a prayer in which the Son renders his final ministerial report to the Father and then intercedes for those who have been put in his pastoral care. Our passage covers only the first part of the prayer.

Once again we must contend with the Johannine ambivalence according to which Jesus is yet to be glorified and is already glorified; he is still in the world and no longer in the world; his hour has now come and his hour is yet to be fulfilled. Rather than attempt to treat theological exposition as though it were a matter-of-fact reportage of a prayer uttered by the historical Jesus (which would include, in v. 3, his self-identification under the title of Christian faith as "Jesus Christ"), it seems a better course to identify some of the key terms of Johannine theology which are crowded together in this brief passage.

"The hour" of Jesus, which in John 2:4 had not yet come—yet was anticipated in that he then manifested his glory (2:11)—is the moment in which Jesus accomplishes the work which the Father has given him to do. It is in this hour that Jesus glorifies God and in turn is glorified by him: it is a manifestation of the glory shared by Father and Son before the world was made (v. 5), a shared life which, through the sending of the Son into the world, is now a communicated life (eternal life to all whom the Father has given to the Son, v. 2). Put in other words, it is the manifestation of God's name (v. 6). ("Name," we remember, is for John the person's self and the experience of that person, as in 14:13–14.) Or in still other words, it is for the Son to give to the chosen the words given to him by the Father (vv. 7–8), which he now prays that they may keep (cf. 14:23–24). The variety of figures underscores the one reality: in the Christ of the church, in his profession and in his teaching, is to be found the one source of eternal life, the only life that counts, the life which is communion with God.

HOMILETICAL INTERPRETATION

Jesus' goings are as odd as his comings. Coming in a feeding trough, he leaves on a cloud—dubious entries and exits to say the least. But Jesus' departure is a beginning for us, and like his, our going will be rough. Yet, our going begins in prayer. Many in the church today don't know whether they are coming or going. They are so immersed in activities that they lose all sense of purpose. Perhaps the reason is that they have forgotten to begin with prayer. Every ministry and every day should start on its knees. Today, Christ prays for us and we pray for the coming of the Spirit. When the going gets rough (and it will), we can pray in the midst of suffering.

First Lesson: Acts 1:1–14. Stopping on a crowded street corner and staring up is bound to entice others to look up out of curiosity. Yet in this scene, only the eyes of faith will see what's happening. Remember standing at the window waving good-bye to someone you love as the plane leaves the ground? Luke spares us these details, these feelings. All we get is the facts. A novelist would do more, but with a different purpose in mind. For Luke, Jesus is gone and we must go. And that's about it. So move off the street corner before you get a crick in your neck. Move back to the upper room to wait and pray. Some young Christians wear buttons with a single index finger pointing up, saying "one way." Christ may go up one way on ascension day, but at the same moment God's power descends upon us in his Spirit. Ascent and descent. We separate those events by days and by seasons, but they are concurrent in our lives and in the church. So the button reads "one way" (up) while the symbol for the Spirit is a dove pointing down. Of course, Christ's *up* and the Spirit's *down* mean going *out* for us. David Read calls it "unfinished Easter." But before we set out, we wait and pray—back to the upper room where it all started. Do you see what's happening? Worship leads us into the world. The upper room leads to the street. Mission begins in prayer.

Second Lesson: 1 Pet. 4:12–19. Luke's tidy scene of the first congregation with everybody happy, bent in penitence and up in praise, is made realistic by the experience of these Asia Minor Christians. First Peter is a good corrective for Luke's idealism and optimism. Jesus may have been crucified, raised, and exalted, and we may be bursting with hope as we pray, but that does not change the fact that the world refuses to hear our gospel. Luke's pretty picture is tainted by the brushstrokes of persecution. Christians of all ages have confronted deaf ears and quick tempers. "The world is not ready to hear" is no new claim. The world will never be ready. What is different for us is that we are neither whipped nor chained. Our suffering is more subtle and cruel—we are ignored by the world. Maybe this silent rebuke is what has turned us from the streets back to the upper room. Certainly we are called not to develop a martyr complex but to spread the word of Christ's love, realizing that many will neither hear nor heed it.

There's another word about suffering here. Certainly all suffer; but not every ache and pain means suffering for the Kingdom. None of us is called to be a hypochondriac for Christ. Likewise, not everyone in jail suffers "for Christ." Not everyone caught cheating by the IRS suffers "for Christ." On the other hand, we can live with "undeserved" suffering because of Christ. Here *live* means more than the secular *cope*. Even more, in the midst of suffering, the question from another, "Why do you smile?" becomes an opportunity for evangelism.

Gospel: John 17:1–11. James Dickey writes in *God's Images,* "He lifted away from me easily. . . . He entered the cloud. He was gone from us, and never gone. Never." Even more than the synoptics, reading John's Gospel is like reading a novel but knowing the last chapter all the way through. Here the risen Christ, the glorified Christ, is gone, but not gone; in fact, "never gone," really. Before we wait and pray, before we move out and meet persecution, we hear our Lord pray. He prays for us and suffers for us. He not only offers up this prayer but he offers up himself in sacrifice, for the "hour" has come. Christ our High Priest becomes the sacrifice. Somehow we see for the first time what Christ has been up to, what the Father has been up to. When you stand too close to an impressionistic painting you see only part of the artist's idea. Stand back from this prayer and you will see more, more than a Johannine "sign" now.

Notice also how Christ prays for us before he prays for the world. In today's passages we see two views of the world. One in Acts where the world is to be converted; another in 1 Peter and John where the world is hostile. Here we can face the world's hostility and the world's indifference because Christ has already faced it and died doing so. We go not knowing where in the world we are going, but knowing confidently that we go with Christ.

We began this season by saying that Easter was the beginning of something big. Now we stand on the brink of something bigger as the church is propelled into the world. After Golgotha we waited, stunned and broken. Now after the ascension we wait stunned but emboldened—another meaningful pause in the church year. We wait in prayer. We wait breathlessly for the coming of the Spirit.